Clear Grammar 1

Clear Grammar 1

Activities for Spoken and Written Communication

Keith S. Folse

Ann Arbor

THE UNIVERSITY OF MICHIGAN PRESS

Acknowledgments

I would like to thank the numerous professionals who gave their expert advice in the design of the grammar presentations and some of the activities used in this textbook. Among these professionals, I would especially like to acknowledge members of TESLMW-L (the materials writers group on the TESL-L electronic communication list) who offered suggestions. Both TESL-L and TESLMW-L have proven time and time again to be excellent sources of new teaching ideas and techniques.

Special thanks go to the professionals at ESL programs at the following schools who contributed ideas and suggestions for the design and content of this book: American Language Academy (Seattle), American Language Academy (Tampa), ESL (Seattle), Houston Community College, Loyola University (New Orleans), Oregon State University (Corvallis), San Francisco State University, Spring Hill College (Mobile, AL), Tulane University (New Orleans), the University of Central Florida (Orlando), the University of Monterrey (Monterrey, Mexico), the University of North Texas (Denton), the University of South Florida (Tampa), the University of Southern Mississippi (Hattiesburg), the University of Washington (Seattle), and Valencia Community College, (Orlando).

Finally, I would like to thank the staff of the University of Michigan Press who have worked with me on this project, particularly Mary Erwin and Kelly Sippell.

Contents

To the Teacher

Clear Grammar 1 is part of a three-volume series of grammar books for beginning to low-intermediate level students of English as a second or foreign language. Book 1 covers the basics of English for nonnative speakers, including the verb *to be*, regular verbs, simple present, simple past (regular and some irregular forms), present progressive, *yes-no* questions, negation, demonstrative words, possessive words, *wh-* questions, word order, quantity words, and prepositions.

Clear Grammar 2 continues with more difficult points, including irregular past tense, articles, and modals. *Clear Grammar 3* concludes this series with present perfect, infinitives vs. gerunds, and relative clauses.

Clear Grammar 1 contains exercises that provide relevant practice in the basic grammar points for beginning students of English as a second language (ESL). It assumes that the student has at least basic reading and writing ability with the English alphabet. It is designed to be used by adult learners, that is, high school age and up. It is suitable for either intensive or nonintensive programs.

An important feature of this book is the number and variety of types of exercises included. Teachers and learners need a large number of practices. A plus of this book is that it contains more than 160 exercises and activities. Furthermore, whenever possible, two smaller exercises have been included instead of one long exercise so that one may be done in class with the teacher's guidance and the other can be sent home for independent learning. A second advantage of this book is the variety of types of practice exercises and learning activities. For example, approximately 20 percent of the exercises are speaking or some type of interaction activities. Some grammar points can be practiced at the single-sentence level while other points may be learned better if seen within a larger context. A strong attempt has been made to provide engaging activities in addition to the traditional single sentences with one blank. To this end, the written exercises are fairly equally divided between sentence-level exercises and multisentence- and dialogue-level activities. Therefore, the resultant structure of this book is 20 percent speaking/interactive exercises, 40 percent single-sentence practices, and 40 percent multisentence or minidialogue activities.

These last figures clearly illustrate an extremely important difference between the *Clear Grammar* series and other grammar books. While some grammar ESL books have included some speaking activities and others have included a few multisentence-exercises, the three books in this series make use of contextualized exercises where possible. These features represent current views toward the learning of grammar in a second language, namely that speaking practice is as important as written practice and that some grammar points are more apparent to students when these points are seen within a real and somewhat longer context.

Clear Grammar 1 has six main goals:

1. to teach the basic grammar points necessary for beginning ESL students;
2. to provide ample written practice in these structures at the single-sentence level as well as at the multisentence and dialogue levels;
3. to provide a wide array of practices at varying cognitive levels (i.e., not just knowledge and comprehension but also synthesis and evaluation);
4. to provide oral communication work practicing these structures through a variety of activities and games;
5. to provide ample opportunities for students to check their progress while studying these structures; and
6. to serve as a grammar reference that is written with language and terms that a beginning-level ESL student can understand without teacher assistance.

Clear Grammar 1 consists of twelve units. Each unit covers a single grammar point, but sometimes one point may have subdivisions. An example is unit 8, "Word Order," in which the sequencing of adverbs of place before adverbs of time is followed by a discussion of adjectives before nouns in English. Another example is unit 11, "Prepositions," which teaches the use of three prepositions for place and for time.

In addition to the twelve core units, there is a pre-unit that introduces three grammar terms that are the smallest amount of terminology that a student will need to succeed in this book, namely *noun, verb,* and *adjective*. While grammar terminology is avoided for the most part, terms for these basic parts of speech as well as a grasp of their meaning are necessary.

The units may be done in any order. However, it is recommended that the general sequencing of the units be followed whenever possible. An attempt has been made to recycle material from one unit into following units where appropriate. For example, once past tense for regular verbs has been covered, many of the sentences in subsequent exercises (e.g., unit 11 on prepositions) include past tense for further reinforcement.

Though a great deal of variety of material exists in the book, there is a general pattern within each unit. The units begin with some kind of grammar presentation. Sometimes this presentation is inductive; other times it is deductive. This presentation is then followed by a list of the most likely mistakes (i.e., potential problems) for each structure. This is followed by a series of written exercises arranged from least to most cognitively demanding. After the written work are one or more speaking activities. This is followed by a multiple choice quiz. At the end of each unit there is a review test.

General Lesson Format

1. Grammar Presentation

    These presentations vary in method. In some units, they are deductive; in others, inductive; and in others, consciousness raising. L2 learners have a wide range of learner styles and employ an even greater range of learner strategies. It is believed that having a variety of presentation types for the grammatical structures is therefore advantageous.

2. List of Potential Errors with Corrections

    In this section of the unit, there is a list of several of the most commonly made errors. Right after each error is the corrected form so that students can see not only what they should avoid but how it should be corrected. Our students represent a wide range of linguistic groups, and every effort has been made to take this into account in selecting which kinds of errors to include here.

3. Written Exercises

   Teachers and students want a large number of written exercises to allow for ample practice of the newly learned structure. The exercises have been sequenced so that the early exercises require only passive knowledge of the grammar point. For example, students circle one of two answers or put a check mark by the correct word. These exercises are followed by others that are more cognitively demanding and require active production of the language structure. In this way, students can comfortably move from passive knowledge to active production of a structure.

   The written exercises in this book are short enough to be done in a small amount of time, yet they are thorough enough to provide sufficient practice for the structure in question. These exercises may be done in class or as homework. Furthermore, they may be checked quickly either by individual students or by the class.

4. Speaking Activities

   Each unit has at least one (and often several) speaking activities. The instructions are clearly written at the top of the exercise. Students are often directed to work with a partner. In this case, it is important for the teacher to make sure that students do not see their partner's material ahead of time as this will not be conducive to facilitating speaking. (However, not all speaking activities are set up in this manner. See the directions for the individual exercises for further clarification.)

5. Multiple Choice Exercise

   Because students often have such a hard time with this particular format and because it is similar to the format found on many standardized language tests, each unit includes an eight-question multiple choice exercise. It is important to discuss not only why the correct answers are correct but also why the distractors are not correct.

6. Review Test

   Equally as important as the teaching of a given grammar point is the measurement of the learning that has taken place. To this end, the last exercise in most units is a review test. This review test has several *very* different kinds of questions on it. For example, one kind of question may require a simple completion while another may require error identification. This variety allows all students an opportunity to demonstrate their knowledge without interference caused by the type of question.

Answer Key

In the back of the book, there is a section that contains the answers for all exercises in this text. These answers are provided so that students may check to see if their answers are correct. It is supposed that students will use the answer key after they have actually done the exercises. It is further hoped that students will use the answer key to detect their mistakes and then return to the exercises to discover the source of their error. The answer key also makes it possible for students engaged in independent study to use this workbook.

Grammar Terminology

In this book, grammar is not viewed as a theoretical science that requires complex terminology. Surely the main purpose of studying grammar in a foreign language is to be able to function better in that language, that is, to produce *accurate* communication (not just communication). To that end, the main focus of the presentations in this book is on being able to use English accurately and not on learning labels that are of little use. However, this does not mean that terminology is or should be avoided. Before unit 1, there is a short pre-unit that teaches the basics of nouns, verbs, and adjectives. In other units, terms such as *direct object* and *possessive pronoun* are introduced and explained. However, grammar terminology is only introduced when it is necessary. Furthermore, when it is introduced, explanations have been simplified to reflect the level of the learner's English ability. Complex grammar terminology serves no justifiable purpose and is to be avoided at all costs in good ESL classes and materials.

Using This Book in Your Curriculum

The number of hours needed to complete this book depends to a large extent on the students in your class. A beginning-level group may need up to 60 hours to finish all the material, while a more advanced group might be able to omit certain units and do more work as homework, therefore using less class time. In this case, the students could finish the material in approximately 35 hours. The results of the diagnostic test (at the end of the book) can help you decide which units, if any, can be omitted or should be assigned as homework to certain students only in order to use group class time the most effectively.

Another factor that will greatly influence the number of class hours needed to complete this material successfully is whether or not the oral activities are done in class. It is recommended that teachers make every effort to do these speaking fluency activities in order to build up students' speaking ability and their confidence in their ability to use spoken English. An instructor in a course in which time is an important factor should consider ways of correcting student homework quickly (e.g., posting homework answer sheets on the wall) that are less time consuming rather than omitting the speaking fluency activities.

There is a diagnostic test at the back of the book. More information about this test is given in the next section. In order to make the best use of (limited) class time, the results of this test can guide you in choosing which units to cover and which units may be omitted.

About the Diagnostic Test

The diagnostic test is printed on perforated pages. Have the students remove this test and take it at the first class meeting. The test consists of twenty-two questions, two for each of the eleven units. (The twelfth unit of the book is a review of the entire book, and thus no question matches it solely.) The test is set up in two parts, each part consisting of eleven questions. You may set your own time limit, but a recommended time limit is twenty minutes.

The scoring for the test is fairly straightforward. On the test sheet, look to see for which units the student has missed both questions, for which units the student has missed only one of the two questions, and for which units the student has not missed either of the questions. You will need to make a composite picture of the results for your whole group. The units for which the most students have missed both questions or one question are the units that your class should focus on first.

Testing

Evaluation is extremely important in any language classroom, and it has a definite role in the grammar classroom. Frequent testing, not just major exams but small quizzes or checks, is vital to allow the learners to see what they have mastered and what still needs further work and to facilitate the teacher in gauging whether individual students have understood and retained the contents of the class.

Testing can come in many forms. Some teachers prefer cloze activities; others prefer multiple choice. Some teachers prefer discrete grammar items; others insist on context. Some include listening and/or speaking; others deal only with printed language. The most important things to keep in mind when testing are (1) students should know what kind of questions to expect, that is, they should know what they will have to do, because this affects how they should study, and (2) the test should test what was taught and nothing else. This second point is the mark of a good test and is essential to the fair treatment of the students.

About the Final Test

In addition to the diagnostic test, there is a final test on page 195. This is meant to be done toward the end of the course when most, if not all, of the book has been covered. This test is also printed on perforated pages and should be removed early in the course to prevent students from looking ahead. For this reason, some teachers will have students remove this test at the first class meeting and then collect these tests. It is not recommended that the results of this particular test be used as the sole deciding factor in whether a student moves from one level or course to the next. This is especially true if you have not had your students answer this type of question during the course. In general, this type of test is more difficult than regular multiple choice or cloze, and any student who scores at least 70 percent is probably ready to move on to *Clear Grammar 2*.

This test has two parts, each of which has the same directions. Students are to find the grammatical error in each sentence and correct it. Each of the two parts has eleven sentences, one sentence for each of the units in the book (except the review unit, of course). The questions are in numerical order matching the corresponding units in the book. Thus, question number 7 in each part deals with material found in unit 7. It is possible to give the first part of this quiz as a progress check midway through the course and then to give the other half at the end to compare results. Again, it is not recommended that any decision regarding promotion to the next level of study be based solely on the results of this single exam.

Pre-Unit

Beginning Grammar Terms

1. noun   2. verb   3. adjective

Before you begin this book, it is a good idea to make sure that you understand three basic grammar words that you will see many times in this book and in your grammar class. These three words are **noun, verb,** and **adjective.**

Noun   A noun is the name of a person, place, thing, or feeling.

The teacher is standing next to the blackboard. (2 nouns)
New York is a very big city in the northeastern part of the U.S. (4 nouns)
Love is a very strong emotion. (2 nouns)
There is a cat on the table. The cat has long white hair. (4 nouns)

Exercise 1.   Underline the nouns in these sentences. Follow the example.

          example: The student has two green books.

1. John and Mark live in a small apartment in Miami.

2. The best color for a new car is red.

3. That is Mr. Jenks. He is the teacher in my second class.

4. Please sit down in that chair by the window.

5. The weather was hot and humid.

6. Do you have a green sports car?

7. Can you play tennis with me at the park on Monday?

8. There are six books on the desk in the first row.

9. The bus is in the station.

10. The library and the school are next to the lake.

Verb A verb shows action or being. Examples of verbs: **go, do, be, speak.**

Every day I <u>get</u> up, <u>take</u> a shower, <u>get</u> dressed, and <u>go</u> to school. (4 verbs)
New York <u>is</u> a very big city in the northeastern part of the U.S. (1 verb)
Two students <u>are standing</u> next to the blackboard. (1 verb)
She <u>didn't eat</u> anything for breakfast, so now she<u>'s</u> hungry. (2 verbs)

Exercise 2.   Underline the verbs in these sentences. Follow the example.

example: The student <u>has</u> two green books.

1. John and Gordon <u>live</u> in a small apartment in Miami.

2. The best color for a new car <u>is</u> red.

3. That <u>is</u> Mr. Jenks. He <u>teaches</u> my second class.

4. Please <u>sit down</u> in that chair by the window.

5. The weather <u>was</u> hot and humid.

6. Which book <u>is</u> your book?

7. He <u>played</u> tennis five hours yesterday, so today he<u>'s</u> really tired.

8. The telephone book <u>is</u> on the desk.

9. Ian <u>drives</u> buses. He's a bus driver.

10. I <u>don't like</u> apples, so please <u>give</u> me an orange.

Adjective An adjective describes a noun. It tells something about the noun.

The <u>young</u> teacher is standing next to the <u>big</u> blackboard. (2 adjectives)
New York is a very <u>big</u> city in the <u>northeastern</u> part of the U.S. (2 adjectives)
<u>Real</u> love is a very <u>strong</u> emotion. (2 adjectives)
There is a cat on the table. The cat has <u>long</u> <u>white</u> hair. (2 adjectives)

Exercise 3.   Underline the adjectives in these sentences. Follow the example.

example: The student has two green books.

1. John and Mark live in a <u>small</u> apartment in Miami.

2. The <u>best</u> color for a new car is <u>red.</u>

3. That is Mr. Jenks. He is the teacher in my <u>second class.</u>

4. Please sit down in the chair <u>by the window</u>.

5. Summer weather in Florida is <u>hot</u> and <u>humid</u>.

6. I think the <u>big</u> painting in the bedroom is very <u>beautiful</u>, but it is so <u>big</u>.

7. Marsha said the test was <u>very</u> difficult.

8. The teacher's book is on the <u>brown</u> desk.

9. The <u>old</u> woman bought five <u>large</u> cans of soup.

10. We live in a <u>large</u>, old house on a <u>small</u>, quiet street.

CAREFUL!

Sometimes a word can be one type of word in one sentence, and the same word can be a different type of word in another sentence. For example, a word can be a noun in one sentence, but then the same word can be an adjective in a different sentence. Look at this example.

- I see a <u>bus</u>. **Bus** is a noun.
- That is the <u>bus</u> station. Here **bus** is an adjective. It tells what kind of station.

In these examples, a word can be a verb in one sentence, but then the same word can be a noun in a different sentence. Look at these examples.
- He <u>is swimming</u> now. **Swimming** is a verb.
- <u>Swimming</u> is good exercise for our bodies. Here **swimming** is a noun.
- Please <u>copy</u> these words five times. **Copy** is a verb.
- Here is a <u>copy</u> of the test for you. Here **copy** is a noun.

Exercise 4.   The underlined word in each group of two or three sentences is the same word, but the part of speech (noun, verb, adjective) is different. Write *n, v,* or *adj* on the line to tell whether the words are nouns, verbs, or adjectives. Follow the example.

example: <u> n </u>   <u>Snow</u> is white.

              <u> v </u>   In the winter, it <u>snows</u> a lot here.

<u> n </u>   1. Nassar is a good <u>cook</u>.

<u> v </u>   2. He doesn't <u>cook</u> meat very well, but he is very good with vegetables and desserts.

<u> a </u>   3. My favorite color for a shirt is <u>light</u> yellow.

<u> n </u>   4. Please turn on the <u>light</u> in the bedroom.

<u>   </u>   5. It's difficult to <u>light</u> a candle when it's windy.

<u> n </u>   6. How much is a <u>pack</u> of paper?

<u> v </u>   7. I'm going to France tomorrow, so tonight I will <u>pack</u> my suitcase.

<u> v </u>   8. Can you <u>telephone</u> me tomorrow night?

<u> n </u>   9. The <u>telephone</u> is on the desk.

<u> a </u>   10. The <u>telephone</u> book is on the desk.

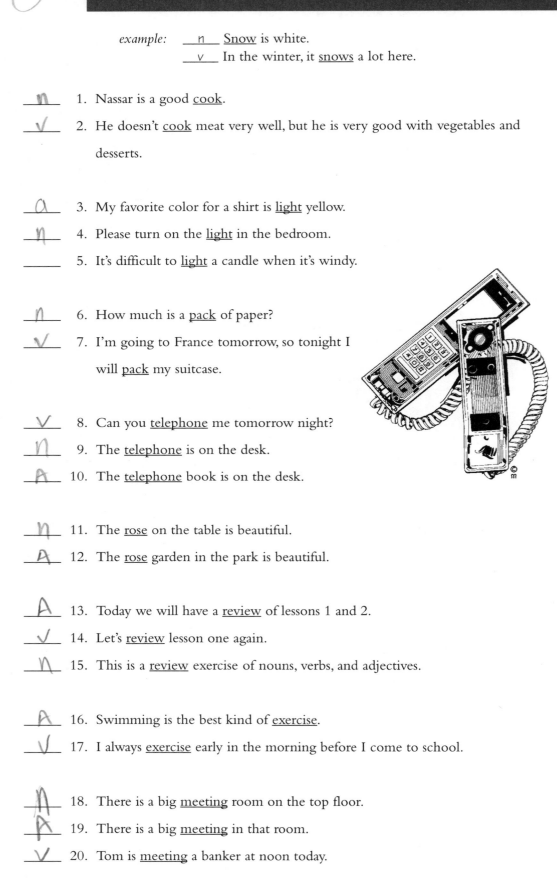

<u> n </u>   11. The <u>rose</u> on the table is beautiful.

<u> a </u>   12. The <u>rose</u> garden in the park is beautiful.

<u> a </u>   13. Today we will have a <u>review</u> of lessons 1 and 2.

<u> v </u>   14. Let's <u>review</u> lesson one again.

<u> n </u>   15. This is a <u>review</u> exercise of nouns, verbs, and adjectives.

<u> a </u>   16. Swimming is the best kind of <u>exercise</u>.

<u> v </u>   17. I always <u>exercise</u> early in the morning before I come to school.

<u> n </u>   18. There is a big <u>meeting</u> room on the top floor.

<u> a </u>   19. There is a big <u>meeting</u> in that room.

<u> v </u>   20. Tom is <u>meeting</u> a banker at noon today.

Unit 1

Present Tense of *Be*

1. simple present tense
2. affirmative
3. negative
4. subject pronouns
5. questions
6. short answers

Simple Present Tense of *Be:* Affirmative

Singular

I **am** in class now.

You **are** here today.

Mike **is** hungry. He **is** in the kitchen.

Pam **is** a good swimmer. She **is** very fast.

The car **is** red. It **is** new.

Plural

The students and I **are** in class.
We **are** in class.

You and Mike **are** friends.
You **are** friends.

Mike and Pam **are** hungry.
They **are** in the kitchen.

Pam and Hank **are** good swimmers.
They **are** very fast.

The cars **are** red. They **are** new.

Grammar

I } am   he, she, it } is   you, we, they } are

In the simple present tense, **be** has 3 forms: **am, is, are.**
    am is used with **I**: I am.
    is is used with **he, she,** or **it**: he is, she is, it is.
    are is used with **you, we,** or **they**: you are, we are, they are.

I, you, he, she, it, we, and **they** are called *subject pronouns.*

CAREFUL! Watch out for these common mistakes.

1. Do not use **am, is,** or **are** with the wrong subject.
    wrong: Joseph and Mark is in the kitchen.
    correct: Joseph and Mark are in the kitchen.

    wrong: Mike and I am hungry now.
    correct: Mike and I are hungry now.

2. Do not omit **am, is,** or **are** from the sentence.
    wrong: India and Pakistan two countries in Asia.
    correct: India and Pakistan are two countries in Asia.

    wrong: The name of the new restaurant on Green Street "The Market."
    correct: The name of the new restaurant on Green Street is "The Market."

Exercise 1.　　Fill in the blanks with the correct forms of *be: am, is, are.*

Simple Present Tense of *Be*

Singular

1. I _am_
2. you _are_
3. he _is_
4. she _is_
5. it _is_

Plural

6. we _are_
7. you _are_
8. they _are_

Exercise 2.　　Underline the correct forms of *be: am, is, are.* Follow the example.

> *example:*　Tanya and Scott (am, is, <u>are</u>) good students.
> Tanya (am, <u>is</u>, are) good at English, and Scott
> (am, <u>is</u>, are) good at math.

1. Yolanda (am, <u>is</u>, are) my best friend. She (am, <u>is</u>, are) 25 years old.

2. Mr. and Mrs. Johnson (am, is, <u>are</u>) good tennis players. Mrs. Johnson (am, <u>is</u>, are) a good swimmer, too.

3. My cats (am, is, <u>are</u>) black and gray. The black cat's name (am, <u>is</u>, are) Coal. The gray cat's name (am, <u>is</u>, are) Smokey. Both cats (am, is, <u>are</u>) very good pets.

4. Mr. and Mrs. Smith have a new house. It (am, <u>is</u>, are) very nice. The living room and the kitchen (am, is, <u>are</u>) very big, but the dining room (am, <u>is</u>, are) small.

5. I (<u>am</u>, is, are) from Colombia. Colombia (am, <u>is</u>, are) a good country. The weather in Colombia (am, <u>is</u>, are) very nice, and the people (am, is, <u>are</u>) nice, too. The main language (am, <u>is</u>, are) Spanish. It (am, <u>is</u>, are) a good place to visit.

Exercise 3.   Fill in the blanks with the correct forms of *be: am, is, are.* Follow the example.

      example: Keith _____is_____ a good tennis player.

1. The weather _____IS_____ very cold today.

2. The most difficult class for me _____IS_____ reading.

3. Jamie and I _____are_____ good swimmers.

4. He _____is_____ in the kitchen right now.

5. Jan and Sue _____are_____ in Japan this week.

6. She _____is_____ a child. She _____is_____ only 8 years old.

7. The president _____is_____ an important person.

8. Michael Jackson _____is_____ a singer.

9. You _____are_____ from a small town, and I _____am_____ from a big city.

10. Sarah and I _____are_____ late to class every day.

11. China _____is_____ a big country.

12. I _____am_____ thirsty. I want some water.

13. German cars _____are_____ expensive.

14. Brazil _____is_____ a country in South America.

15. We worked hard all day today. We _____are_____ tired now.

16. Washington and Florida _____are_____ states in the U.S.

17. I _____am_____ in class at 8 A.M. every day.

18. Mike, Joe, and Susan _____are_____ in the same class.

19. Monday _____is_____ a difficult day for many people.

20. This exercise _____is_____ very easy.

Brazil

Exercise 4.   Write the correct forms of *be: am, is, are.* Follow the example.

      example: Tanya and Scott _are_ good students. Tanya _is_ good at English, and Scott _is_ good at math.

1. Japan and China _____are_____ countries in Asia. China _____is_____ a very large country. Japan _____is_____ smaller than China.

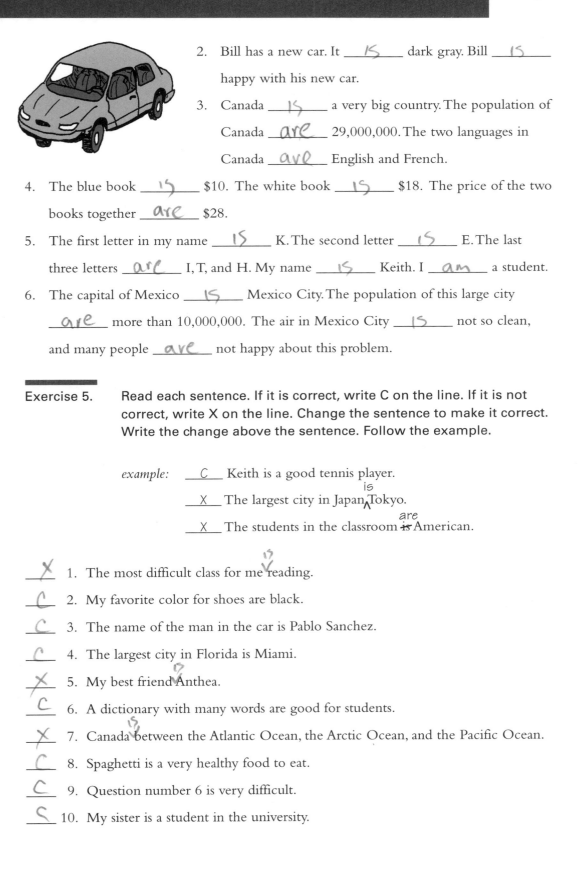

2. Bill has a new car. It ___*is*___ dark gray. Bill ___*is*___ happy with his new car.

3. Canada ___*is*___ a very big country. The population of Canada ___*are*___ 29,000,000. The two languages in Canada ___*are*___ English and French.

4. The blue book ___*is*___ $10. The white book ___*is*___ $18. The price of the two books together ___*are*___ $28.

5. The first letter in my name ___*is*___ K. The second letter ___*is*___ E. The last three letters ___*are*___ I, T, and H. My name ___*is*___ Keith. I ___*am*___ a student.

6. The capital of Mexico ___*is*___ Mexico City. The population of this large city ___*are*___ more than 10,000,000. The air in Mexico City ___*is*___ not so clean, and many people ___*are*___ not happy about this problem.

Exercise 5. Read each sentence. If it is correct, write C on the line. If it is not correct, write X on the line. Change the sentence to make it correct. Write the change above the sentence. Follow the example.

> *example:* ___C___ Keith is a good tennis player.
>
>   *is*
> ___X___ The largest city in Japan ^ Tokyo.
>
>   *are*
> ___X___ The students in the classroom ~~is~~ American.

  is
___X___ 1. The most difficult class for me ~ reading.

___C___ 2. My favorite color for shoes are black.

___C___ 3. The name of the man in the car is Pablo Sanchez.

___C___ 4. The largest city in Florida is Miami.

  is
___X___ 5. My best friend ~ Anthea.

___C___ 6. A dictionary with many words are good for students.

  is
___X___ 7. Canada ~ between the Atlantic Ocean, the Arctic Ocean, and the Pacific Ocean.

___C___ 8. Spaghetti is a very healthy food to eat.

___C___ 9. Question number 6 is very difficult.

___C___ 10. My sister is a student in the university.

Exercise 6.   Speaking Activity: *Be* Verb Drill. Do student A OR student B. Do *one* of these only.

Step 1.   Number the left lines from 1 to 10 in any order. Mix up the numbers.
Step 2.   Fill in the right lines with *am, is,* or *are.* Check your answers with another student who did the same part (A or B) as you did.
Step 3.   Work with a partner who did not do the same part as you. Student A will read out all ten items as quickly as possible in numerical order. Student B must close the book and listen and then complete the items correctly. For example, student A will say, "you," and student B must say, "you are." If this is correct, student A says, "That's correct." If this is not correct, student B says, "Try again" and repeats the item. When all the items are finished, student B will read out the other ten items.

Follow the examples.

> *examples:*   he = he __is__
>   John and Carol = John and Carol __are__

Student A

___. you = you __are__

___. the girl = the girl __is__

___. the cat = the cat __is__

___. today = today __is__

___. Eric = Eric __is__

___. Joe and Pam = Joe and Pam __are__

___. my car = my car __is__

___. the boys = the boys __are__

___. dinner = dinner __is__

___. Toronto = Toronto __is__

Student B

___. he = he __is__

___. Rachel = Rachel __is__

___. the cats = the cats __are__

___. we = we __are__

___. the shoes = the shoes __are__

___. the teacher = the teacher __is__

___. Brazil = Brazil __is__

___. the boy = the boy __is__

___. I = I __am__

___. the weather = the weather __is__

Exercise 7.   Writing and Speaking Practice

Part 1.   In each sentence, there is one difference from the previous sentence. Look at the change. Write the correct form of *be: am, is, are.*

Beginning sentence: Susan is here now.

1. I   I __am__ here now.

2. you   You __are__ here now.

3. they   They __are__ here now.

4. at school   They __are__ at school now.

5. Mr. Lim   Mr. Lim __is__ at school now.

6. a teacher   Mr. Lim __is__ a teacher now.

7. I   I __am__ a teacher now.

8. Jim   Jim __is__ a teacher now.

9. Jim and I   Jim and I __are__ teachers now.

10. here   Jim and I __are__ here now.

11. Susan   Susan __is__ here now.

12. I   I __am__ here now.

Part 2.   Speaking Practice. Now work with a partner. One person closes the book. The other student reads the beginning sentence "Susan is here now." Then that student reads the words after each number, and the second student has to say the new sentence. For example, for number 1 student A will say, "I," and student B should say, "I am here now." Do all twelve of the sentences. When you finish, change roles. Try to work as quickly as possible.

Simple Present Tense of *Be:* Negative

Singular

I **am not** in class now.

You **aren't** sick today.

Mike **isn't** tall. He is short.

Jo **is not** a good swimmer.
She **isn't** very fast.

The car **isn't** red. It **is not** new.

Plural

The students and I **are not** in class.
The students and I **aren't** in class.

You and Mike **aren't** friends.
You **are not** friends.

Mike and Pam **aren't** hungry.
They **are not** in the kitchen.

Pam and Hank **aren't** good swimmers.
They **are not** very fast.

The cars **are not** red. They **aren't** new.

To make a negative statement with **am, is,** or **are,** add the word <u>not</u> after **am, is,** or **are.**

It is also possible to use contractions (= short forms) with **is** and **are: is not** OR **isn't; are not** OR **aren't.** There is no contraction for **am not.**

Karla **is** hungry. Peggy **is not** hungry. (OR: Peggy **isn't** hungry.)
The shirts **are** cheap. They **aren't** expensive. (OR: They **are not** expensive.)
A tiger **is** a dangerous animal. A tiger **is not** a small animal. (OR: **isn't**)
He **is** from New York. He **isn't** from Chicago. (OR: **is not**)
I **am** happy. I **am not** sad. (no contraction possible)

Grammar

I } **am not**   he
she } **is not**   you
it } **(isn't)**   we } **are not**
they } **(aren't)**

In the simple present tense, **be** has three negative forms: **am not, is not (isn't), are not (aren't).**

    am not is used with **I:** I am not.
    is not is used with **he, she,** or **it:** he is not, she is not, it is not.
    (**isn't** is also OK: he isn't, she isn't, it isn't.)
    are not is used with **you, we,** or **they:** you are not, we are not, they are not.
    (**aren't** is also OK: you aren't, we aren't, they aren't.)

CAREFUL! Watch out for these common mistakes.

1. Do not forget to use **be (am, is, are).**
    wrong: I not very tired now.
    correct: I am not very tired now.

    wrong: California, Texas, and Alaska not small states.
    correct: California, Texas, and Alaska aren't small states. (OR are not)

2. Do not say **no am** or **no is** or **no are.** Say **am not, is not (isn't),** or **are not (aren't).**
    wrong: The food at that restaurant no is good.
    correct: The food at that restaurant isn't good. (OR is not)

    wrong: The apples on the tree no are red.
    correct: The apples on the tree are not red. (OR aren't)

Exercise 8. Read each sentence. Some verbs need to be changed to negative verbs to make the sentences correct. Cross out the verbs that must be changed and write the negatives above. Follow the examples.

example: Chicago ~~is~~ ^isn't^ the largest city in the U.S. The largest city in the U.S. is New York City.

1. D is the first letter of the alphabet. The first letter of the alphabet is A. J is the last letter of the alphabet. The last letter of the alphabet is Z.

2. Denise is a girl's name. Dennis is a girl's name. Mark is a boy's name. Marsha is a boy's name.

3. Vegetables are good for our health. A potato is a vegetable. An orange is a vegetable. An onion is a vegetable. A carrot is a vegetable, too.

4. Verbs and nouns are important words. *Cat* is a verb, but *buy* is a verb. *Go* and *stop* are nouns. *Book* and *table* are nouns.

Exercise 9. Complete the sentences with the correct forms. Follow the example.

example: 2 __is__ a number. It __is not__ a big number. It __is__ a small number.

1. Brazil __isn't__ in Africa. It __is__ in South America. It __is__ a big country.

2. I __am not__ an astronaut. I __am__ a student.

3. This exercise __isn't__ very difficult. The answers __is__ easy for me!

4. Some insects __are__ beautiful. For example, a butterfly __is__ very beautiful, but a fly __isn't__ pretty.

5. Africa __isn't__ a country. Africa __is__ a continent. Europe and Asia __is__ continents, too. Brazil and China __isn't__ continents. They __are__ countries.

6. Ontario and Alberta are very big. They __are__ countries. They __aren't__ provinces in Canada.

Exercise 10.   Speaking Activity: Negative *be* Drill (see directions for exercise 6). Fill in the right lines with *am not, isn't,* or *aren't.* Follow the examples.

> *examples:* my car = my car __isn't__
> they = they __aren't__

Student A   *Student B*

___. lunch = lunch __isn't__   ___. I = I __am not__

___. my friends = my friends __aren't__   ___. the weather = the weather __isn't__

___. today = today __isn't__   ___. we = we __aren't__

___. Peter = Peter __isn't__   ___. my shoes = my shoes __aren't__

___. you = you __aren't__   ___. he = he __isn't__

___. the child = the child __isn't__   ___. Katie = Katie __isn't__

___. the cat = the cat __isn't__   ___. Japan = Japan __isn't__

___. my parents = my parents __aren't__   ___. my brother = my brother __isn't__

___. Ben and Ted = Ben and Ted __aren't__   ___. the teacher = the teacher __isn't__

___. the birds = the birds __aren't__   ___. my car = my car __isn't__

Homework suggestion: Have students write complete TRUE sentences using any of the above structures.

> *examples:*   The weather isn't good.
> Japan isn't a flat country.

Making a Question

To make a *yes-no* question, move **am, is,** or **are** to the beginning:

Statement	*Question*
Mark is in the kitchen.	Is Mark in the kitchen?
The shoes are $60.	Are the shoes $60?
I am in your chair.	Am I in your chair?

CAREFUL! Watch out for these common mistakes.

1. Do not begin **am/is/are** questions with **do** or **does.**

   wrong: Do you hungry?
   correct: Are you hungry?

   wrong: Does the weather is hot in your country?
   correct: Is the weather hot in your country?

2. In writing, do not begin **am/is/are** questions with a noun or pronoun. Begin with **am, is,** or **are.**

   wrong: You are hungry?
   correct: Are you hungry?

   wrong: This book is very expensive?
   correct: Is this book very expensive?

Exercise 11.   Make *yes-no* questions from the statements in the four conversations. Follow the example.

        example: *A:* Shopping makes me tired!
        (You are tired.)   *B:* <u>Are you tired?</u>
                            A: Yes, I want to sit down! My feet hurt!

Conversation A

                                      A: What is that?
                                      B: It's a new book. It's called *The Red River.*

1. It is a good book.   *A:* <u>Is it a good book</u>
                                      B: Yes, it's very good. There is a movie, too.

2. The movie is good.   *A:* <u>Is good the movie?</u>
                                      B: The movie is OK, but the book is much
                                          better.

Conversation B

                                      A: Do you know Kevin and Sandra?
                                      B: Yes, they are students at the Language School.

3. They are from Italy.   *A:* <u>Are they from Italy?</u>
                                      B: No, they aren't. They're from France.

4. They are in the same class.   *A:* <u>Are they in the same class</u>
                                      B: No, they aren't. Kevin is in Level 1, and
                                          Sandra is in Level 3.

Conversation C

                                      A: Where is Nancy?
                                      B: She's in the hospital.

5. She's in the hospital again.   *A:* What? <u>Is she in the hospital again?</u>
                                      B: Yes, she is.

6. She's OK.   A: _Is she OK?_
                B: She's all right, but she's in a lot of pain.

7. She's really sick.   A: _Is she really sick_
                B: Well, she has a broken leg. The doctor says that she will be in the hospital for two or three days.

Conversation D   A: United Airlines. May I help you?
                B: Yes, please. Do you fly to Cairo?
                A: Yes, twice a week. When do you want to travel?

8. There is a flight on Monday.   B: Next week. _Is there a flight on Monday?_
                A: Yes, there is.

9. It's in the morning.   B: _Is it in the morning._
                A: Yes it is. You leave at 8 A.M. and arrive in Cairo at 6 P.M. How is that?

                B: That sounds great. I'd like to make a reservation.
                A: Oh, I'm sorry, but that's not possible.

10. The flight is full.   B: Why? _Is the flight full?_
                A: Yes, it is. There aren't any seats now. Can I check another day for you?

Exercise 12.   Scrambled Sentences. Read the words and then make a question. Don't forget to add the question mark (?). Follow the example.

         example: today is tired Greg   _Is Greg tired today?_

1. happy Smith is Mrs. today   _Is Mrs. Smith happy today?_
2. cats now thirsty the are   _Are the cats thirsty now?_
3. Paul in and Naomi class today are   _Are Paul and Naomi in class today?_
4. now cold weather is the   _Is the weather cold now?_
5. homework his correct is   _Is his homework correct?_
6. day you late class to are every   _Are you late to class every day?_
7. Venezuela Caracas capital is the of   _Is the Caracas the capital of Venezuela?_
8. open Ben on the Street now is bank   _Is the bank on the Ben Street open now?_
9. Saturday park crowded is on the   _Is the park crowded on Saturday?_
10. sleepy today Sam and Vick are   _Are Sam and Vick sleepy today?_
11. busy is the now teacher very   _Is the teacher very busy now?_
12. is Robert day early to class every   _Is Robert early to class every day?_

Exercise 13. Write the correct words *(am, is, are)* in the blanks to make questions and answers in these conversations. Draw a line (—) if you do not need to write a word. Follow the example.

> *example:* A: " _Are_ Henry and Paul _—_ good baseball players?"
> B: "No, they _aren't_ good players. They _aren't_ good at baseball."

1. A: " _Is_ today _—_ Monday?"

   B: "Yes, today _Is_ Monday."

   A: "Really? I can't believe it!"

2. A: " _Are_ your name _—_ Mario?"

   B: "No, it _isn't_. My name _Is_ Mark."

   A: "Oh, I _am_ sorry."

3. A: " _Is_ Amalia _—_ hungry now?"

   B: "Yes, she _Is_ very hungry. She wants to eat two Big Macs!"

   A: "Really? I _'m_ surprised. Amalia _Is_ so thin. I can't believe she can eat two Big Macs!"

4. A: " _Are_ we _—_ in the correct classroom?"

   B: "Yes, I think so. I think this _Is_ the right room."

5. A: " _Are_ you _—_ 25 years old?"

   B: "Yes, I _am_. Why?"

6. A: " _Are_ cats _—_ dangerous?"

   B: "No, they _aren't_. Cats _are_ good pets."

Short Answers

To answer a *yes-no* question, use **am, am not, is, isn't, are,** or **aren't** in your answer.

question:	Are you hungry now?
full answer:	Yes, I am hungry now.
	(OR: Yes, I'm hungry now.)
	No, I am not hungry now.
short answer:	Yes, I am.
	No, I am not.

question:	Are the apples fresh?
full answer:	Yes, the apples are fresh.
	No, the apples aren't fresh.
short answer:	Yes, they are.
	No, they aren't.

CAREFUL! Watch out for these common mistakes.

Do not forget **am, is,** or **are** in the short answer for **am/is/are** questions.

wrong:	Is Nancy home now? Yes, she home.
correct:	Is Nancy home now? Yes, she is.

wrong:	Are the students happy about their scores. No, they not.
correct:	Are the students happy about their scores? No, they aren't.

Exercise 14. Write the two possible short answers for each question. Follow the example.

example: Is your reading class easy?
   __Yes, it is__ . OR __No, it isn't__ .

1. Are cats good pets for children?
   __Yes, they are__ . OR __No, they aren't__

2. Are Sam, Mark, and Ron in the same class this year?
   __Yes, they are__ . OR __No, they aren't__

3. Are you sleepy?
   __Yes, I am__ . OR __No, I'm not__ .

4. Is the food at that restaurant delicious?
   __Yes, it is__ . OR __No, it isn't__ .

5. Are you and Gina on different softball teams?
   __Yes, we are__ . OR __No, we aren't__

6. Is China the biggest country in the world today?
   __Yes, it is__ . OR __No, it isn't__ .

7. Is the teacher the tallest person in the classroom?
   __Yes, he is__ . OR __No, he isn't__ .

8. Are coffee and tea good for your health?
   __Yes, they are__ . OR __No, they aren't__ .

9. Is the homework for this class very difficult?

   <u>Yes, it is</u>. OR <u>No, it isn't</u>.

10. Is Jack in the kitchen now?

   <u>Yes, he is</u>. OR <u>No, he isn't</u>.

Exercise 15.   Speaking Activity. Work with a partner. Each student chooses one "mystery friend." Your job is to guess the name of your partner's mystery friend. Take turns asking *yes-no* questions about the mystery friend. If the answer is *yes*, the questioner continues asking questions. If the answer is *no*, the partner can ask questions. The first person to guess the partner's mystery friend is the winner. Follow the examples.

examples of questions: Is your friend a woman?

                             Is your friend short?

                             Is she tall?

possible answers: Yes, he is. Yes, she is. No, he isn't. No, she isn't.

Kevin	*Carl*	*Melissa*	*Brenda*
a man	a man	a woman	a woman
tall	short	tall	short
from Florida	from Florida	from Florida	from Florida
a bus driver	a taxi driver	a bus driver	a taxi driver
Alan	*Mark*	*Terri*	*Jeanine*
a man	a man	a woman	a woman
tall	short	tall	short
from Florida	from Florida	from Florida	from Florida
a taxi driver	a bus driver	a taxi driver	a bus driver
Mario	*Victor*	*Chanda*	*Theresa*
a man	a man	a woman	a woman
tall	short	tall	short
from New York	from New York	from New York	from New York
a bus driver	a taxi driver	a bus driver	a taxi driver
Scott	*Lee*	*Shelley*	*Lori*
a man	a man	a woman	a woman
tall	short	tall	short
from New York	from New York	from New York	from New York
a taxi driver	a bus driver	a taxi driver	a bus driver

More practice: Do this activity again with another student. This game has some luck, but some students are good players. Have a competition among the students in your class to see who the best guesser is.

──────────

Exercise 16.   Multiple Choice. Circle the letter of the correct answer.

1. "Where are the books?"

    "Well, the grammar book is on the sofa, and the vocabulary book and the reading

    book __*are*__ on the table."

    (A) is   (C) isn't

    (B) are   (D) aren't

2. The name on all of the books _____ "Mary D. Smith."

    (A) are   (C) is

    (B) am   (D) not

3. "Are you and Mike friends?"

    "Yes, _____."

    (A) I am   (C) you are

    (B) we are   (D) he is

4. "The questions are difficult."

    "Yes, _____ very hard."

    (A) they are   (C) are

    (B) it is   (D) is

5. "Where are the boys?"

    "Joseph and Mark _____ in the kitchen."

    (A) is   (C) are

    (B) no is   (D) no are

6. "Do you think grammar class is difficult?"

    "No, it isn't. The most difficult class _____."

    (A) reading is   (C) reading

    (B) is reading   (D) I think

7. "_____ cheap in your country?"

"No, they aren't. They're very expensive."

  (A) Cars are   (C) Are cars

  (B) Gasoline is   (D) Is gasoline

8. "Are you from Asia?"

"No, _____."

  (A) you are   (C) you aren't

  (B) we are   (D) we aren't

Exercise 17.   Review Test

Part 1. Read this short passage. Fill in the blanks with *am, is,* or *are.*

This _is_ a map of North America. The country to the north of the United States _is_ Canada. Canada _is_ a very large country, but not so many people live in Canada. The population _are_ 29,000,000. (The population of the United States _are_ 265,000,000.)

Canada has two official languages. These two languages _are_ English and French. Most of the people who speak French live in Quebec. Quebec _is_ a large province in Canada. (A province _is_ similar to a state.)

The capital of Canada _is_ Ottawa. The largest cities _are_ Toronto, Vancouver, and Montreal. Vancouver _is_ in the west, but Toronto and Montreal _are_ not in the west. Montreal _is_ in the eastern part of the country, and Toronto _is_ in the central part of Canada.

Part 2. Read this short passage. There are six mistakes. Circle the mistakes and write the correct form above each mistake.

My son's name is Chris. Chris ten years old. He is in the fifth grade in elementary school. He likes to study. Is a good student.

My daughter's name Jenny. Jenny is seven years old. She in the second grade in school elementary. Chris and Jenny is in the same school, but they are in different grades.

Part 3. Read each sentence carefully. Look at the underlined part. If the underlined part is correct, circle the word *correct*. If it is wrong, circle the wrong part and write the correct form above.

correct wrong   1. Brazil <u>is</u> a very big country in South America.

correct wrong   2. <u>Miss Miller a teacher</u> at the high school.
                         Miss Miller is a teacher

correct wrong   3. The green book and <u>the yellow notebook are on the table</u>.

correct wrong   4. Kennedy <u>is</u> a name that everyone knows.

correct wrong   5. I want to buy a new car, but <u>the price very expensive</u>.
                         the price is very expensive

correct wrong   6. The pencils <u>no are</u> here.
                         aren't

correct wrong   7. I want to eat a big cheeseburger because <u>I am</u> hungry.

Unit 2

Present Tense of Regular Verbs

1. simple present tense
2. affirmative
3. negative
4. questions
5. short answers

My daily routine

I get up at 7:00 A.M.

get

I eat a big breakfast.

eat

I walk to work.

walk

I work from 8 to 4.

work

I come home at 4:30.

come

VERB

My father's daily routine

He gets up at 6:45 A.M.

gets

He eats a light breakfast.

eats

He drives to work.

drives

He works from 7:45 to 2.

works

He comes home at 2:30.

comes

VERB+s

23

Discover Grammar

1. Look at the box below. Circle all the verbs on the left side of the box and on the right side of the box. Do not circle forms of *be*. There are thirteen verbs.

2. Are the two groups of verbs the same? _____

    _____

3. What is different? _____

    _____

4. Can you explain this difference? _____

    _____

[Check page 42 for the answer to these questions.]

Present Tense of Verbs

I, you, we, they + VERB

I live in an apartment.
You come to class on time every day.
Nadine and Cassandra work in the day.
The U.S. and Mexico have long coasts.
We do our homework after school.

A: Are you and Jim students?
B: Yes, we are. We have 4 classes.

he, she, it + VERB + s

Jennifer lives in a small house.
He sometimes comes to class late.
Mike works at night.
Canada has long coasts.
Todd does his homework at night.

A: Wow! Is that your cat? It's so fat!
B: Yes, it eats a lot. It likes fish the best.

Now look at these examples.

		EAT	WRITE	STUDY	GO	HAVE
I		I eat	I write	I study	I go	I have
you	VERB	you eat	you write	you study	you go	you have
we		we eat	we write	we study	we go	we have
they		they eat	they write	they study	they go	they have
he		he eats	he writes	he studies	he goes	he has
she	VERB + s	she eats	she writes	she studies	she goes	she has
it		it eats	it writes	it studies	it goes	it has
				y — i(+es)	o(+es)	has

In the present tense, a verb has 2 forms: **VERB** or **VERB** + **s.**
VERB is used with **I, you, we,** and **they.**
VERB + **s** is used with **he, she,** and **it.**

CAREFUL! Watch out for these common mistakes.

1. Use **VERB** + **s** when the subject is **he, she,** or **it.**
   wrong: Laura cook scrambled eggs for breakfast every day.
   correct: Laura cooks scrambled eggs for breakfast every day.

   wrong: Canada have two official languages.
   correct: Canada has two official languages.

2. Remember to change **y** to **i** and add **es.**★ Remember to add **es** after **o, sh, ch,** and **ss.**
   wrong: My baby sister crys when she is hungry.
   correct: My baby sister cries when she is hungry.

   wrong: Zina dos the dishes after dinner.
   correct: Zina does the dishes after dinner.

3. Use only **VERB** (no **s**) when the subject is **I, you, we,** or **they.**
   wrong: Collin and Laura cooks scrambled eggs for breakfast every day.
   correct: Collin and Laura cook scrambled eggs for breakfast every day.

   wrong: Paraguay and Canada has two official languages.
   correct: Paraguay and Canada have two official languages.

4. Do not use **be** with verbs in simple present tense.
   wrong: I am walk to school every day.
   correct: I walk to school every day.

   wrong: He is speak English and Chinese.
   correct: He speaks English and Chinese.

★ We don't change **y** to **i** if the letter before **y** is a vowel (**a, e, i, o, u**).
  examples: say, says; enjoy, enjoys; buy, buys; BUT cry, cries; study, studies

Exercise 1. Fill in the blanks with the correct forms of the verbs. Follow the examples.

SPEAK	WATCH	DO	TRY
I _speak_	I _watch_	I _do_	I _try_
you (sing.) _speak_	you _watch_	you _do_	you _try_
he _speaks_	he _watchs_	he _does_	he _tries_
she _speaks_	she _watchs_	she _does_	she _tries_
it _speaks_	it _watchs_	it _does_	it _tries_
we _speak_	we _watch_	we _do_	we _try_
you (pl.) _speak_	you _watch_	you _do_	you _try_
they _speak_	they _watch_	they _do_	they _try_
Jo _speaks_	Jo _watchs_	Jo _does_	Jo _tries_
Jo and I _speak_	Jo and I _watch_	Jo and I _do_	Jo and I _try_
you and I _speak_	you and I _watch_	you and I _do_	you and I _try_

TAKE	PLAY	HAVE	BE
I _take_	I _play_	I _have_	I _am_
you (sing.) _take_	you _play_	you _have_	you _are_
he _takes_	he _plays_	he _has_	he _is_
she _takes_	she _plays_	she _has_	she _is_
it _takes_	it _plays_	it _has_	it _is_
we _take_	we _play_	we _have_	we _are_
you (pl.) _take_	you _play_	you _have_	you _are_
they _take_	they _play_	they _have_	they _are_
Jo _takes_	Jo _plays_	Jo _has_	Jo _is_
Sue and Jo _take_	Sue and Jo _play_	Sue and Jo _have_	Sue and Jo _are_
you and I _take_	you and I _play_	you and I _have_	you and I _are_

Exercise 2.   Underline the correct form of each verb. Follow the example.

     example: You (<u>live</u>, lives) near my house.

1. Mr. Smith (play, <u>plays</u>) tennis every morning. He (play, <u>plays</u>) with Mr. Gonzalez. Both of them (<u>enjoy</u>, enjoys) this sport very much.

2. I (<u>do</u>, does) my math homework with a pencil. This is because sometimes I (<u>make</u>, makes) mistakes. My friend Brenda is the opposite. She rarely (make, <u>makes</u>) mistakes. She (use, <u>uses</u>) a pen for her math homework.

3. Laura and Ellen (<u>work</u>, works) in the same office. Laura (work, <u>works</u>) in the morning, and Ellen (work, <u>works</u>) in the afternoon. They (<u>work</u>, works) from Monday to Friday.

4. Mrs. Keats is a good cook. She sometimes (try, <u>tries</u>) new kinds of food. She (like, <u>likes</u>) to cook fried chicken or chicken with vegetables.

5. Our class (begin, <u>begins</u>) at 8:30. The teacher (arrive, <u>arrives</u>) at 8:15, and the students (<u>come</u>, comes) to class between 8:20 and 8:30. The teacher (like, <u>likes</u>) the students to arrive on time. If a student (come, <u>comes</u>) late, the teacher (get, <u>gets</u>) angry.

6. Brian (work, <u>works</u>) at the bank. He (finish, <u>finishes</u>) work at 5:30. Then he (go, <u>goes</u>) home. He (watch, <u>watches</u>) the news on TV at 6:00. After that, he (eat, <u>eats</u>) dinner. Sometimes his friend Zina (come, <u>comes</u>) to his house. Sometimes Brian and Zina (<u>watch</u>, watches) movies on TV.

Exercise 3.   Fill in the blanks with the correct forms of the verbs. Follow the example.

     example: (have)   Anne <u>has</u> a new TV.

1. (play)   Neil and Steve sometimes <u>play</u> tennis at the university.

2. (have)   Vancouver <u>has</u> the second largest Chinatown in North America. (The largest Chinatown in North America is in San Francisco. New York has the third largest.)

3. (speak)   Sandra <u>speaks</u> four languages.

4. (take)   This machine <u>takes</u> coins and paper money.

5. (need)   Lynn and Pat <u>need</u> help with their homework.

6. (come)   I never <u>come</u> to class late.

7. (drink)   My sister <u>drinks</u> orange juice with milk.

8. (drink)   My sister and my mother ___drink___ three cups of

coffee in the morning.

9. (explain) The teacher ___explains___ the lesson.

10. (ask)   The students ___ask___ questions.

11. (answer) The teacher ___anwers___ the students' questions.

12. (be)   Mr. Giles ___is___ a businessperson.

Exercise 4.   Write a verb on each line. Sometimes more than one answer is correct. Follow the example.

> *example:*   Maria _____ three languages.
> (Possible answers are: studies, speaks, practices, needs)

1. All new cars today ___have___ seat belts. They ___are___ very safe.

2. I usually ___watch___ TV in the morning, but my cousin ___watchs___ TV at night. She ___has___ a black and white TV. It ___is___ very old. I ___have___ a color TV. It ___is___ new.

3. Paula ___is___ a student. She ___sleeps___ every night. She ___make___ her homework every night. She ___is___ a good student.

4. Sometimes I ___help___ Tina with her homework, and sometimes she ___helps___ me with my homework.

5. Ben ___is___ a good swimmer. He ___is___ very fast.

6. Jason and Karen ___are___ in this house. They ___like___ this house very much. The house ___haves___ three bedrooms, two bathrooms, a kitchen, and a living room. The bedrooms ___are___ very big, but the kitchen ___is___ small. Karen and Jason ___watch___ TV in the living room every evening.

7. Caroline Andrews ___works___ from 8:00 A.M. to 3:00 P.M. five days a week. She ___is___ a teacher. She ___teachs___ math at an elementary school. She ___lives___ very far from the school. Every morning she ___leaves___ her house at 7:15. She ___goes___ to school. This ___are___ about 30 minutes. She ___is___ at school at 7:45. Her first class ___is___ at 8:30.

Exercise 5.   Speaking Activity: Conjugation Game

Step 1. Choose six verbs from the list below.
Step 2. Write the verbs on the top lines. Then write the correct forms for each subject in the columns.
Step 3. Work with a partner. Say your first verb. Your partner must say all the correct forms of the verb. Then your partner says his or her first verb. You must say all the correct forms of the verb. Take turns doing this.

Verbs					
arrive	begin	come	drink	eat	have
leave	like	live	practice	pronounce	sing
speak	study	teach	understand	work	read
write	play	visit	want	learn	listen
repeat	talk	open	close	walk	run
do	send	take	think	make	call
be	go	use	type	wash	erase
catch	watch	know	get	need	

1. leave   2. begin   3. make   4. have   5. pronounce

I	leave	begin	make	have	pronounce
you (sing.)	leave	begin	make	have	pronounce
he	leaves	begins	makes	has	pronounces
she	leaves	begins	makes	has	pronounces
it	leaves	begins	makes	has	pronounces
we	leave	begin	make	have	pronounce
you (pl.)	leave	begin	make	have	pronounce
they	leave	begin	make	have	pronounce

Homework: Write three *original* sentences using the verbs above.

1. _____

2. _____

3. _____

Present Tense of Verbs: Negative

I, You, We, They

Affirmative

I **like** tennis.
I **have** a car.

You **speak** French.
You **read** well.

We **live** in an apartment.
We **watch** TV at night.

They **swim** in the pool.
They **eat** a big lunch.

Negative

I **do not like** football.
I **don't have** a bicycle.

You **do not speak** Chinese.
You **don't read** badly.

We **don't live** in a house.
We **do not watch** TV in the morning.

They **don't swim** in the river.
They **do not eat** a big dinner.

He, She, It

He **speaks** French.
He **has** a radio.

She **does** the dishes.
She **writes** many letters.

It **rains** a lot in April.
It **costs** $10.

He **does not speak** Spanish.
He **doesn't have** a TV.

She **doesn't do** her homework.
She **doesn't write** many postcards.

It **doesn't rain** a lot in October.
It **does not cost** $20.

To make a negative statement with a verb, add **do not** OR **does not** before the verb.

It is also possible to use contractions (= short forms): **do not** OR **don't; does not** OR **doesn't.**

Grammar

I
you
we   } + { do not
they   (don't) } + **VERB**

he
she   } + { does not
it   (doesn't) } + **VERB**

In the present tense, a verb has two negative forms: **do not (don't), + VERB, does not (doesn't) + VERB.**

Do not is used with **I, you, we,** or **they:** I do not, you do not, we do not, they do not. (**Don't** is also OK: I don't, you don't, we don't, they don't.)

Does not is used with **he, she,** or **it:** he does not, she does not, it does not. (**Doesn't** is also OK: he doesn't, she doesn't, it doesn't.)

CAREFUL! Watch out for these common mistakes.

1. Do not forget to use **don't (do not)** or **doesn't (does not)**.
   wrong: I not speak French well.
   correct: I do not speak French well. (OR don't)

   wrong: The U.S. no have 100 states.
   correct: The U.S. doesn't have 100 states. (OR does not)

2. Do not use **am not, isn't,** or **aren't** with a verb. Use **don't** or **doesn't** only.
   wrong: The man isn't like this food.
   correct: The man doesn't like this food. (OR does not)

   wrong: Nell and Vick aren't play tennis every day.
   correct: Nell and Vick do not play tennis every day. (OR don't)

3. Do not use **s** with the verb for **he/she/it.** You need **s** for **he/she/it** only one time
   in the verb. If you have **does,** then the verb doesn't have **s.**
   wrong: He doesn't likes coffee.
   correct: He doesn't like coffee.

   wrong: It doesn't smells good.
   correct: It doesn't smell good.

Exercise 6.   Fill in the blanks with the correct negative forms of the verbs.
Follow the examples.

LIKE	GO	DO	STUDY
I _don't like_	I _____	I _____	I _____
you (sing.) _don't like_	you _____	you _____	you _____
he _doesn't like_	he _____	he _____	he _____
she _doesn't like_	she _____	she _____	she _____
it _doesn't like_	it _____	it _____	it _____
we _don't like_	we _____	we _____	we _____
you (pl.) _don't like_	you _____	you _____	you _____
you and I _don't like_	you and I _____	you and I _____	you and I _____
they _don't like_	they _____	they _____	they _____
Jo _doesn't like_	Jo _____	Jo _____	Jo _____

KNOW	GET	HAVE	BE
I _____	I _____	I _____	I _____
you (sing.) _____	you _____	you _____	you _____
he _____	he _____	he _____	he _____
she _____	she _____	she _____	she _____
it _____	it _____	it _____	it _____
we _____	we _____	we _____	we _____
you(pl.) _____	you _____	you _____	you _____
they _____	they _____	they _____	they _____
Jo _____	Jo _____	Jo _____	Jo _____
Jo and Sue _____	Jo and Sue _____	Jo and Sue _____	Jo and Sue _____

Exercise 7.   Underline the correct negative form of each verb. Follow the example.

> *example:*   Mary's car is old. She (don't , <u>doesn't</u>) have a new car.

1. The students (don't, doesn't) have class now.

2. Jonathan (don't, doesn't) speak French.

3. Students (don't, doesn't) go to class on Sunday.

4. In North America, people (don't, doesn't) drive on the left side of the road.

5. In Canada and the U.S., people (don't, doesn't) use Mexican pesos or Japanese yen.

6. Muslims★ (don't, doesn't) eat pork.

7. I (don't, doesn't) wear tennis shorts to English class.

8. You (don't, doesn't) arrive in class late.

9. April (don't, doesn't) have 31 days.

10. A year (don't, doesn't) have 400 days.

11. Rick and I (don't, doesn't) understand the teacher's explanation.

12. This food (don't, doesn't) taste good. It is too spicy!†

★ Muslims = members of the Islamic religion
† spicy = hot

Exercise 8.   Fill in each blank with the correct negative form of the given verb. Follow the example.

example: (like) I ___don't like___ fried chicken for breakfast.

1. (go)   Mike and Sam _____ to school by bus. They walk.

2. (drink)   I _____ tea late at night. It has too much caffeine.

3. (have)   The classroom _____ many chairs. It's a small room.

4. (speak)   Philip _____ Spanish. He speaks Portuguese.

5. (take)   She _____ tests with a pencil. She uses a pen.

6. (study)   Angela _____ in the morning. She studies at night.

7. (read)   We _____ in conversation class. We practice speaking.

8. (do)   They _____ their work quickly. They are very slow!

9. (swim)   John is not a good swimmer. He _____ well.

10. (teach)   I teach in the morning. I _____ in the afternoon.

11. (begin)   The class starts at 8:15. It _____ at 8:00.

12. (play)   If the weather is cold, we _____ tennis.

Exercise 9.   Complete each sentence with the negative form of a verb. Sometimes more than one answer is possible. Follow the example.

example: Brenda ___doesn't speak___ English. She is from Venezuela.
             (Other answers are: *doesn't know, doesn't understand*)

1. Cats usually like fish. My cat is a little strange. My cat _____ fried

    fish. Cats usually like milk, too, but my cat _____ milk. Cats usually

    have a long tail, but my cat is different. My cat _____ a long tail. It

    has a very, very short tail.

2. How many letters does the English alphabet have? Some students think the English

    alphabet has 30 letters. This _____ correct. The English alphabet

    _____ 30 letters. There are 26 letters in the English alphabet. Some

    languages have special marks on top of the letters. For example, Spanish has *é* and

    German has *ü,* but English _____ any marks on alphabet letters.

3. Some of my friends use computers to do their homework. I have a computer, but I _____ my homework on a computer. I _____ how to type very well. I prefer to use a pencil when I do my homework.

4. Jody eats all her meals at a restaurant or at her friend's house. She likes to cook, but she never cooks at home. The reason for this is simple. Jody lives in a small apartment, and her apartment _____ a stove, so Jody _____ at home.

5. Many students walk to school. They can do this because they _____ far away. My house is very far from school, so I _____ to school every day.

6. This exercise _____ 20 questions. It has only 6 questions. It _____ difficult. It _____ a long time to do this exercise.

Exercise 10. Write ten negative sentences. *Use a different verb in each sentence.* Write true sentences about yourself, your family, your friends, your things (car, books, dictionary), or your classroom. Follow the examples.

examples: I don't have a car.
              My father isn't 70 years old.

1. _____
2. _____
3. _____
4. _____
5. _____
6. _____
7. _____
8. _____
9. _____
10. _____

After you finish writing your sentences, read your sentences to a partner. Then your partner should read his or her sentences to you. Are there any surprises? Are there any interesting sentences?

Making a Question

Do   A *yes-no* question with **I, you, we,** or **they** begins with **do:**

Statement	*Question*
I talk fast.	Do I talk fast?
You like black coffee.	Do you like black coffee?
We have two classes together.	Do we have two classes together?
Pam and Tony live on Green Street.	Do Pam and Tony live on Green Street?

Does   A *yes-no* question with **he, she,** or **it** begins with **does:**

Statement	*Question*
Paul lives in New York.	Does Paul live in New York?
She has a new car.	Does she have a new car?
It rains a lot in summer.	Does it rain a lot in summer?

CAREFUL! Watch out for these common mistakes.

1. Remember to use **does** with **he, she,** and **it.** Use **do** with other subjects.
    wrong: Do Mary have a new car?
    correct: Does Mary have a new car?

    wrong: Does you like hockey?
    correct: Do you like hockey?

2. Do not put **s** on the verb in *yes-no* questions. Use only the base (simple) form of the verb. For **he/she/it,** you need only one **s** in the question.
    wrong: Does Valerie goes to class every day?
    correct: Does Valerie go to class every day?

    wrong: Does the car has a good radio?
    correct: Does the car have a good radio?

3. Do not begin present tense verb questions with **am, is,** or **are.**
    wrong: Are you speak English?
    correct: Do you speak English?

    wrong: Is Mary have a new car?
    correct: Does Mary have a new car?

Exercise 11. Underline the correct word to begin each question. Follow the example.

> *example:* *A:* "(<u>Do</u>, Does) Fred and Tim live in the same apartment?"
> *B:* "Yes, they are roommates."

1. *A:* "(Do, Does) you understand this lesson?"

   B: "Yes, I do. I think it's an easy lesson."

2. *A:* "(Do, Does) that toy use 4 batteries?"

   B: "Yes, it uses 4 batteries. (Do, Does) you have 4 batteries?"

   A: "No, I don't."

   B: "You have to buy some then."

   A: "(Do, Does) you know a place where I can buy batteries?"

   B: "Yes, go to Target. They sell batteries there."

3. *A:* "(Do, Does) April have 31 days?"

   B: "No, it doesn't have 31 days. It only has 30."

4. *A:* "(Do, Does) you drive a red car?"

   B: "Yes, I drive a red car."

5. *Husband:* "(Do, Does) I snore?"

   Wife: "Yes, you snore very loudly!"

6. *A:* "(Do, Does) you understand the difference between *do* and *does*?"

   B: "I think so. *Does* is for *he, she,* and *it*. And *do* is for *I, we, you,* and *they.*"

Exercise 12. Write the correct words on the lines. Follow the example.

> *example:* (like) _____Do____ you ____like___ coffee with sugar and milk?

1. (have) _____ Matt _____ a dark blue car?

2. (play) _____ you _____ tennis very well?

3. (rain) _____ it _____ a lot in this area in the summer?

4. (study) _____ she _____ English every night?

5. (want) _____ Mary and Jack _____ more coffee now?

6. (read) _____ you _____ at night before you go to sleep?

7. (take) _____ you _____ a shower at night or in the morning?

8. (drive) _____ people in Japan _____ on the right or on the left?

9. (cook) _____ Paul _____ his own food?

10. (speak) _____ Paul and John _____ French?

11. (have) _____ you and John _____ a class together?

12. (go) _____ this bus _____ to Miami?

Exercise 13. Write the correct words on the lines. Follow the example.

example: (write)   Q: __Does Mary write__ letters in the morning?
A: No, __she doesn't write__ letters in the morning.
__She writes__ letters at night.

1. (eat) Q: _____ you _____ cake with a spoon?

A: No, _____ cake with a spoon.

_____ cake with a fork.

2. (go) Q: _____ she _____ to school by car?

A: No, _____ to school by car.

_____ by bike.

3. (do) Q: _____ he _____ his homework on a computer?

A: No, _____ his homework on a computer.

_____ his homework with a pencil.

4. (have) Q: _____ your new house _____ 4 bedrooms and 1 bathroom?

A: No, _____ 4 bedrooms and 1 bathroom.

_____ 3 bedrooms and 2 bathrooms.

5. (speak) Q: _____ Mr. and Mrs. Wilson _____ Arabic?

A: No, _____ Arabic.

_____ English and Spanish only.

Exercise 14.   Read the answer, and then write the question. Use the subjects from the box. Use each subject only *one* time.

a cheeseburger	police in England	banks
you and your family	Mr. and Mrs. Caruthers	it
~~your telephone~~	a police officer	I

1. *Q:* <u>Does your telephone have a fax?</u>

    A: No, it doesn't have a fax.

2. *Q:* _____

    A: No, he or she doesn't wear blue jeans.

3. *Q:* _____

    A: No, they don't have guns.

4. *Q:* _____

    A: Yes, we live in a very old house.

5. *Q:* _____

    A: Yes, it gets very cold in the winter.

6. *Q:* _____

    A: Yes, they have many children.

7. *Q:* _____

    A: No, they don't open on Sundays.

8. *Q:* _____

    A: Yes, you eat too much!

9. *Q:* _____

    A: Yes, it costs one dollar.

Short Answers

To answer a *yes-no* question, use **does, doesn't, do,** or **don't** in your answer.

question:	Do you speak Chinese?
full answer:	Yes, I speak Chinese.
	No, I don't speak Chinese.
short answer:	Yes, I do.
	No, I don't.

question:	Does this word mean "difficult"?
full answer:	Yes, this word means "difficult."
	No, this word doesn't mean "difficult."
short answer:	Yes, it does.
	No, it doesn't.

CAREFUL! Watch out for these common mistakes.

1. Do not use **am/is/are** as a short answer for **do/does** questions.
   - wrong: Does Nancy have a blue car? Yes, she is.
   - correct: Does Nancy have a blue car? Yes, she does.

   - wrong: Do Bolivia and Switzerland have beaches? No, they aren't.
   - correct: Do Bolivia and Switzerland have beaches? No, they don't.

2. Be careful with the verb **have.**
   - wrong: Do you have a car? Yes, I have.
   - correct: Do you have a car? Yes, I do.

   - wrong: Does Canada have states? No, it hasn't.
   - correct: Does Canada have states? No, it doesn't.★

★Canada doesn't have states. Canada has provinces.

Exercise 15. Write the two possible short answers for each question. Follow the example.

example: Does Keith play tennis every day?
   Yes, he does. OR _No, he doesn't_.

1. Do people in that country speak English?

   _____. OR _____.

2. Does it snow in your country?

   _____. OR _____.

3. Does your brother play hockey?

   _____. OR _____.

4. Do you and Ben have math class together?

   _____. OR _____.

5. Does that word mean twelve?

   _____. OR _____.

6. Do I have your book?

    _____. OR _____.

7. Does the teacher arrive at class on time?

    _____. OR _____.

8. Does an orange have a lot of vitamin C?

    _____. OR _____.

Exercise 16.   Speaking Activity. Interview a classmate. Write five original questions using *do/does.* Then ask someone your questions. Write down the answers. Write good questions. Don't write questions that are very easy. Learn new information about your classmate. For example, don't ask, "Do you study English?" because you know the answer. Follow the example.

> *example:*   _Do you cook your own food?_
> _No, I don't. I am not a good cook._

1. *Q:* _____?
    A: _____.
2. *Q:* _____?
    A: _____.
3. *Q:* _____?
    A: _____.
4. *Q:* _____?
    A: _____.
5. *Q:* _____?
    A: _____.

Exercise 17.   Multiple Choice. Circle the letter of the correct answer.

1. "_____ 'elephant' mean a kind of animal?"

    "Yes, that's correct. It's a large gray animal."

    (A) Does   (C) Do

    (B) Is   (D) Are

2. His last name _____ 12 letters. It only has 11.

   (A) don't has   (C) doesn't have

   (B) doesn't has   (D) don't have

3. "Do you and your brother work at the same place?"

   "No, we don't. I work at Nations Bank, and my brother _____ at First Bank."

   (A) work   (C) don't work

   (B) works   (D) doesn't work

4. "Are you and Jim students?"

   "Yes, we _____. We have 3 classes."

   (A) students   (C) he and I

   (B) do   (D) are

5. "_____ the movie have a happy ending?"

   "I don't want to tell you that. It's a surprise."

   (A) Does   (C) Do

   (B) Is   (D) Are

6. Jennifer _____ Arabic very well.

   (A) studys   (C) don't read

   (B) doesn't knows   (D) writes

7. "Is Tom a good student?"

   "No, he isn't. He _____."

   (A) don't have a book   (C) don't do his homework

   (B) doesn't try hard   (D) doesn't studies much

8. "_____ a garage?"

   "Yes, and it's a very big garage."

   (A) Is your new house has   (C) Is your new house have

   (B) Does your new house has (D) Does your new house have

Exercise 18.   Review Test

Part 1. Fill in each blank with any word that makes sense.

I don't like winter. Summer is my favorite season. I _____ like winter for four

reasons. First, the weather in winter _____ very nice. Second, the trees _____

have leaves, and the grass _____ green. Finally, the days _____ long.

Susan is my best friend. She is different from me. She and I _____ have the same

opinion about the seasons. She likes winter very much. She likes cold weather. She

_____ like warm weather. Her favorite sport is skiing, so she _____ happy in

June or July.

Susan _____ like spring, and I have the same opinion. I _____ like spring.

In the spring, it rains a lot. The sun _____ shine for two or three days sometimes.

The rain is good for the plants, but it _____ good for us.

Part 2. Read this short passage. There are five mistakes. Circle the mistakes and
write the correct form above the mistake.

Some of the classes at my school are very large, but my class doesn't very large. There

are only 12 students in my class. The students don't from the same country. They are from

three countries. Seven of the students are from Japan, three are from Mexico, and two are

from Egypt. All of the students don't speak the same language. Their languages no are the

same. Some of the students speak Spanish, some of them speak Japanese, and some of them

speak Arabic. The students from Mexico aren't speak Arabic, and the students from Japan

doesn't speak Spanish.

Part 3. Read each sentence carefully. Look at the underlined part. If the underlined
part is correct, circle the word *correct*. If it is wrong, circle the wrong part
and write the correct form above.

correct   wrong   1. Brazil <u>doesn't</u> a very big country in Asia.

correct   wrong   2. Our houses <u>aren't</u> near the bank.

correct   wrong   3. Marsha <u>no has</u> much money.

correct   wrong   4. The student from Colombia <u>don't speak</u> French.

correct   wrong   5. The state of Florida <u>is not</u> cold in the winter.

correct   wrong   6. Brown and gray <u>doesn't is</u> happy colors.

Answers to DISCOVER GRAMMAR from page 24:

1. (left) live, come, work, home, do, have; (right) lives, comes, works, has, does, eats, likes
2. No, they are not the same.
3. The verbs in the right box finish with the letter *s*.
4. We add an *s* to the verb if the subject of the verb is *he, she,* or *it.*

Unit 3

Demonstratives

1. this   2. that   3. these   4. those

This, That, These, Those

	Singular	Plural
Near the speaker	this _____	these _____
Not near the speaker	that _____	those _____

Demonstrative Adjectives

In these examples, **this, that, these,** and **those** are adjectives. They are used in front of a noun.

Singular
This book is green.
I don't know **this** word.

That apple is fresh.
He watched **that** movie.

Plural
These books are green.
I don't know **these** words.

Those apples are fresh.
He watched **those** movies.

Demonstrative Pronouns

In these examples, **this, that, these,** and **those** are pronouns.★ They are used in place of a noun.

Singular
This is a green book.
I don't know **this**.

That is fresh.
He watched **that**.

Plural
These are green books.
I don't know **these**.

Those are fresh.
He watched **those**.

★**This, that, these,** and **those** are called **demonstratives** in grammar.

CAREFUL! Watch out for these common mistakes.

1. Do not use **this** or **that** with plural examples.
2. Do not use **these** or **those** with singular examples.

wrong:　　　This books are excellent.
correct 1:　This book is excellent. (one book)
correct 2:　These books are excellent. (two or more books)

wrong:　　　That are delicious.
correct 1:　That is delicious. (one kind of food)
correct 2:　Those are delicious. (one or more kinds of food)

Exercise 1.　　Write *this, that, these,* or *those* on the lines. Follow the examples.

Near the Speaker (= here): *this* or *these*

1. _____this_____ student

2. _____these_____ people

3. _____ book

4. _____ green book

5. _____ expensive green book

6. _____ books

7. _____ green books   9. _____ weather

8. _____ expensive green books 10. _____ questions

Not near the Speaker (= there): *that* or *those*

11. _____that_____ man   16. _____ difficult question

12. _____those_____ people   17. _____ questions

13. _____ woman   18. _____ difficult questions

14. _____ nice people   19. _____ words

15. _____ question   20. _____ brilliant idea

––––––––––
Exercise 2.   Write *this, that, these,* or *those* on the lines. Follow the examples.

    examples: (here)   _____This___ cat is very old.
               (there)   _____Those___ cats are not old.

1. (here)   _____ books are green.

2. (here)   Is _____ paper the best?

3. (there)   _____ cats are very beautiful.

4. (here)   In _____ class, we have two tests every week.

5. (there)   _____ cat is pregnant.★

6. (here)   Peter likes _____ car the best. It's really nice.

7. (there)   Are _____ stamps rare? They're really beautiful.

8. (here)   We have _____ kind of fruit in my country, too.

9. (there)   _____ people are from France.

10. (there)   I think _____ questions are really difficult.

11. (here)   _____ computer is easy to use.

12. (there)   _____ nine books are not for you and me.

13. (there)   _____ students are from Spain.

14. (there)   _____ pants are not cheap.

15. (here)   Do you like _____ movie?

★going to have babies, going to be a mother

Exercise 3.   Fill in the second blank in each item with one of the nouns. Use a demonstrative in front of the noun. (Sometimes more than one noun is possible.) Follow the examples.

Near the Speaker

test – diamond – cheeseburger

1. _____This_____ _____diamond_____ is very expensive.

2. _____These_____ _____diamonds_____ are very expensive.

3. _____ _____ is very difficult.

4. _____ _____ are very difficult.

5. _____ _____ are delicious.

Not near the Speaker

trip – table – sandwich

6. _____ _____ is very tiring.

7. _____ _____ are heavy.

8. _____ _____ is heavy.

9. _____ _____ are really hot.

10. _____ _____ is really hot.

Exercise 4.   Write *this, that, these,* or *those* on the lines.

> *Situation:*   The teacher is standing in front of the room. He is at the blackboard. Joe is a student. He is sitting in the back of the room. There is a small box on his desk.

Teacher: Joe, what is _____ on your desk?

Student: What do you mean?

Teacher: _____ box! What is in _____ box?

Student: I brought _____ box from home.

Teacher: Yes, but what is in _____ box?

(Joe puts his hand in the box. He takes out some coins and holds them up for the teacher to see.)

Teacher: What are _____?

Student: _____ are coins. _____ coins are special. They are very old.

Teacher: Please put _____ back in the box. It's time for class now. Perhaps we can all see your coins later, OK?

Exercise 5.   Speaking Activity

Step 1.   There are forty nouns in this box. Choose any twenty-eight of them. Write the nouns on the second line in each pair of lines in the charts below.
Step 2.   Write the correct demonstrative adjective in front of the noun.
Step 3.   Work with a partner. Tell your partner the box (near or not near the speaker) and the noun. Your partner must say the correct demonstrative adjective with your noun.

example: *A:* houses, not near the speaker
            B: those houses
            A: That's correct. Now it's your turn to ask me.
            B: violin, near the speaker
            A: that violin
            B: No, try again. violin, near the speaker
            A: this violin
            B: Yes, that's correct. Now it's your turn to ask me.

apple, apples	family, families	lamp, lamps	table, tables
book, books	guy, guys	name, names	umbrella, umbrellas
cat, cats	house, houses	pencil, pencils	woman, women
desk, desks	job, jobs	radio, radios	year, years
egg, eggs	key, keys	shoe, shoes	zebra, zebras

Near the Speaker

Singular		*Plural*	
demonstrative	+ noun	demonstrative	+ noun
_____	_____	_____	_____
_____	_____	_____	_____
_____	_____	_____	_____
_____	_____	_____	_____
_____	_____	_____	_____
_____	_____	_____	_____
_____	_____	_____	_____

Not near the Speaker			
Singular		*Plural*	
demonstrative	+ noun	demonstrative	+ noun
_____	_____	_____	_____
_____	_____	_____	_____
_____	_____	_____	_____
_____	_____	_____	_____
_____	_____	_____	_____
_____	_____	_____	_____
_____	_____	_____	_____

Exercise 6.   Multiple Choice. Circle the letter of the correct answer.

1. "Do you like this _____?"

   "Yes, very much."

   (A) people   (C) cats

   (B) movies   (D) book

2. "The teacher wrote a word on the board. Can you see it?"

   "No, I can't. What is _____ word?"

   (A) this   (C) that

   (B) these   (D) those

3. _____ do not look good together.

   (A) These painting and those vase   (C) These painting and that vase

   (B) This painting and those vase   (D) This painting and that vase

4. "Excuse me. How much are _____?"

   "They're only five dollars each."

   (A) those   (C) this shirt

   (B) that   (D) these shirt

5. Joe and Sue are outside. There is something strange in the sky. Joe points to the sky.

   Joe: "Hey, Sue, look up in the sky. What _____?"

   Sue: "I don't know. Is it a UFO?"

   (A) is this   (C) are these

   (B) is that   (D) are those

6. Joe and Sue are in a store. Sue picks up a tennis ball and asks Joe about it.

   Sue: "Hey, Joe. What kind of ball is _____?"

   Joe: "That's a tennis ball. You don't play tennis?"

   (A) this   (C) these

   (B) that   (D) those

7. _____ are very good together.

   (A) This table and that chairs   (C) These table and these chairs

   (B) That table and these chairs   (D) Those table and this chairs

8. "Here are some cookies from my mother. Do you want one of _____ cookies?"

   "Yes, I'm really hungry."

   (A) these   (C) those

   (B) this   (D) that

Exercise 7.   Review Test

Part 1.   Read the situation. Then write *this, that, these,* or *those* on the lines.

> *Situation:* Neil is shopping with Paul. They are in a clothing store. Neil sees a shirt behind the counter. The clerk is standing near the shirt. Neil talks to Paul about the shirt. Paul is standing near Neil. Then Neil points to the shirt and asks the clerk a question.

Neil: Paul, do you like _____ shirt over there?

Paul: Which shirt do you mean? There are shirts all over this store.

Neil: _____ one over there. It's the light blue one behind the counter.

Paul: Well, _____ shirt is very nice, but how much is it?

Neil: I don't know. Wait a minute and I'll find out.

Neil: Excuse me. How much is _____ light blue shirt?

Clerk: You mean _____ one here?

Neil: Yes, _____'s the one.

Clerk: It's twenty dollars.

Neil: OK. I'll take one. I need a size 16.

Part 2.   Read each sentence carefully. Look at the underlined part. If the underlined part is correct, circle the word *correct*. If it is wrong, circle the wrong part and write the correct form above.

correct	wrong	1. She really likes those blue <u>shirt</u> very much.
correct	wrong	2. Is <u>these</u> book about the war between those two countries?
correct	wrong	3. The students in <u>those</u> class had very high scores on the test.
correct	wrong	4. <u>This exercise</u> is not very difficult.
correct	wrong	5. <u>That cars are</u> really expensive.
correct	wrong	6. Rain again? I don't like <u>this</u> weather!
correct	wrong	7. The dentist has an office in that <u>building</u> over there.

Unit 4

Possessive Adjectives

1. my
2. your (sing.)
3. his
4. her
5. its
6. our
7. your (pl.)
8. their

Possessive Adjectives	
Subject Pronouns	*Possessive Adjectives*
I	my
you (singular)	your
he	his
she	her
it	its
we	our
you (plural)	your
they	their

I	I play tennis. I have a racket.	**my**	This is my racket. My racket is new.
you (sing.)	You sing well. You are very good.	**your (sing.)**	Your voice is nice. What is your favorite song?
he	He is French. He is from Paris.	**his**	His hair is brown. I don't know his name.
she	She has a car. She drives it to work.	**her**	That is her car. Her car is dark gray.
it	It is my pet. It is a small bird.	**its**	Its name is Jo-Jo. Its tail is bright red.
we	We live here. We are students.	**our**	Our house is big. Do you like our pool?
you (plural)	"Mr. and Mrs. Wilson, do you have children?"	**your (plural)**	"Mr. and Mrs. Wilson, do your children go to River Elementary School?"
they	They play tennis. They play well.	**their**	Their rackets are new. Their coach is good.

Subject pronouns: **I, you** (singular), **he, she, it, we, you** (plural), **they**
We use these before a verb. I like tennis. OR They have a car.

Possessive adjectives: **my, your** (singular), **his, her, its, our, your** (plural), **their**
(M<u>y</u> ends in **y,** hi<u>s</u> ends in **s;** you<u>r</u>, he<u>r</u>, ou<u>r</u>, thei<u>r</u> end in **r**.)
We use these before a noun. My car is green. OR They use my car.

CAREFUL! Watch out for these common mistakes.

1. Do not use subject pronouns before nouns.
    wrong: I book is on the table.
    correct: My book is on the table.

    wrong: They names are Troy and Drew.
    correct: Their names are Troy and Drew.

2. Do not use possessive adjectives without a noun.
    wrong: Where is her?
    correct: Where is her pencil? OR Where is her desk?

    wrong: This is their.
    correct: This is their picture. OR This is their car.

Exercise 1. Write the correct possessive adjectives on the lines. Follow the examples.

1. you   _your_ book
2. Mary   _her_ book
3. you and Mary   _____ books
4. your wife   _her_ car
5. the man and I   _our_ books
6. the machine   _its_ cord
7. Bob, Jo, and Sue   _____ father
8. my watch   _____ battery
9. they   _their_ mother
10. it   _it's_ tail

11. we   _our_ team
12. the boy   _his_ test
13. the boy   _his_ tests
14. my daughter   _her_ shoes
15. she   _her_ test
16. Alan and Tom   _their_ tests
17. Ann and Mary   _their_ tests
18. Ted, Bob, and I   _our_ tests
19. Ted and Bob   _their_ answers
20. Bob and I   _our_ answers

CHALLENGE A student says the answer for #12 is *his* and the answer for #13 is *their*. One answer is wrong. You are the teacher now. Can you explain the answer here?

Exercise 2. Write the correct possessive adjectives on the lines. Follow the examples.

1. I   _my_ name
2. Tom   _his_ name
3. you and I   _____ books
4. my wife   _____ boss
5. the man   _____ bike
6. you   _____ car
7. the book   _____ cover
8. the car   _____ engine
9. he   _his_ key
10. they   _____ key
11. she   _____ keys
12. she and I   _____ idea

13. she and I   _our_ ideas
14. the cat   _____ tail

The Boss

15. John _____ mother

16. Ann _____ mother

17. Ann and Jo _____ mother

18. Ann and Jo _____ father

19. our parents _____ house

20. he and Ned _____ parents

21. John and I _____ cars

22. the boy _____ hobby

23. you and Jo _____ hobbies

24. your son _____ hobbies

25. Mr. Jones _____ car

26. Mrs. Jones _____ car

27. my sister _____ car

28. his sister _____ car

29. we _____ car

30. the baby _____ name

CHALLENGE   A student says the answer for #20 is *his*. This is wrong.
You are the teacher now. Can you explain the answer here?

Exercise 3.   Underline the correct words. Follow the example.

1. Do you like (I, <u>my</u>) new car?

2. This is (his, he) watch.

3. (They, Their) last name is Smith.

4. Please tell me (your, you) phone
   number.

5. I know (she, her) sister.

6. (Our, We) class begins at 10 A.M.

7. When is (we, our) next test?

8. Bob likes cats. (He, His) pets are all cats.

9. Bob has a cat. (Its, It) name is Red.

10. (My, I) test score is 95.

Exercise 4.   Write the correct possessive adjectives on the lines. Follow the
                   examples.

examples: This cat is very old. ____His____ name is Felix.
               John has a new car. I like ____his____ car very much.

1. *A:*   "When is _____ math class?"

   B: "It's at 9:30."

   A: "Who is _____ teacher?"

   B: "OK, hold on a minute . . . Oh, I can't remember . . . _____ mind is not
          so clear today."

A: "Is _____ teacher a man or a woman?"

B: "Oh, now I remember the teacher's name. _____ name is Mr. Barlow."

A: "Do you think he is a good teacher?"

B: "Well, yes, I do. I like _____ teaching style."

A: "So is this class easy for you?"

B: "Sometimes it's easy, but sometimes it isn't."

A: "Why is that?"

B: "Well, _____ problem is that I like to watch TV. I study when I have to study, but I don't study very much. _____ grades are pretty bad!"

2. *José:* "Rick, do you have an idea for the food for the party?"

   Rick: "Yes, I do. _____ idea is to serve sandwiches."

   José: "Does anyone else have an idea?"

   Rick: "Well, Susan has an interesting idea."

   José: "Really? Susan, what's _____ idea?"

   Susan: "_____ idea is to serve cheeseburgers."

   José: "Wow, that doesn't sound very good for a party.
   Does anyone else have an idea?"

   Susan: "Yes, Ben has an idea."

   José: "Where is Ben?"

   Susan: "I don't know. I'm surprised he isn't here."

   José: "OK, what is _____ idea for the party?"

   Susan: "He wants all the guests to cook _____ favorite food and bring it to the party."

   José: "Oh, right. This is called a potluck dinner in the U.S."

   Rick: "Hey, don't forget Martha and Lim. They have an idea for the party, too.
   _____ idea is to serve pizza."

   José: "I really like pizza. In fact, it's _____ favorite food. I like _____ idea!"

Exercise 5.   Possessive Adjectives and Subject Pronouns. Underline the correct words. Follow the example.

1. (My, <u>I</u>) have a new car.

2. This is (his, he) sweater.

3. (They, Their) last name is Hobbs.

4. (They, Their) are from Ohio.

5. (She, Her) and (she, her) sister are here.

6. (Our, We) begin (we, our) class at 10 A.M.

7. (Our, We) have a test tomorrow.

8. (He, His) likes cats. (He, His) has 5 cats.

9. Bob has a cat. (Its, It) is a female cat.

10. Do (you, your) play tennis every day?

Exercise 6.   Possessive Adjectives and Subject Pronouns. Read each sentence. If it is correct, write C on the line. If it is not correct, write X on the line. Change the sentence to make it correct. Write the change above the sentence. (*Hint:* There are twelve sentences. Four are correct, and eight have mistakes.)

_____   1. I don't like my math teacher.

_____   2. Do your live in an apartment or a house?

_____   3. Is it name Kitty?

_____   4. She and she sister are twins.

_____   5. Samuel is a newspaper delivery person. He brings the newspaper to our house every day.

_____   6. I have math class at 10 A.M., but I first class is at 9 A.M.

_____   7. She is a French teacher. Her name is Mrs. deMontluzin.

_____   8. His is a doctor. He has an office in Miami.

_____   9. Jack and I like bright colors, and we favorite color is yellow.

_____ 10. Keith, Sheila, and Rachel study together. Their are good friends.

_____ 11. Sachiko and Tomoyo are from Japan. They passports are red.

_____ 12. This cake is good. Its main ingredients are flour and sugar.

Exercise 7.   Speaking Game

Step 1.   Work with a partner.
            There are four streets with nine houses on each street, so there are thirty-six houses in the box. Choose one house that is your house. Circle that house. Do NOT let your partner know which house is your house.

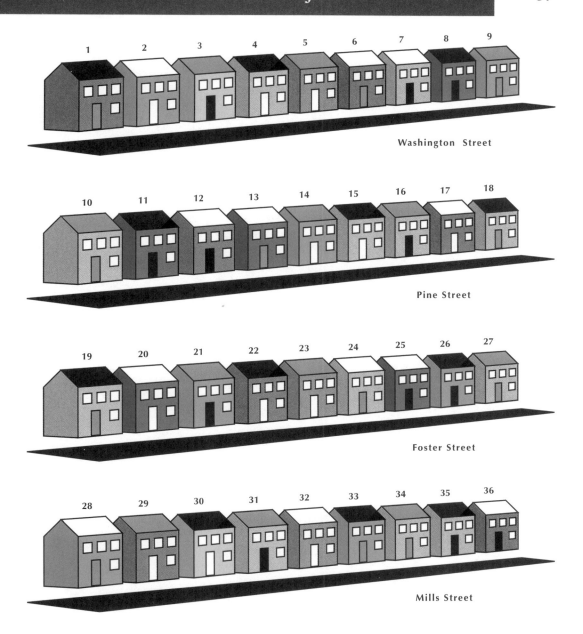

Step 2. Take turns asking *yes-no* questions to try to guess your partner's house. If the answer to a question is YES, then the questioner can continue asking. If the answer is NO, the turn passes to the other student.

Step 3. The first partner to guess the right house is the winner! (You can't use the house numbers until the end!)

example: *A:* Is your house on Mills Street?

B: No, my house isn't on Mills Street. (So it's B's turn to ask a question.)

B: Is your house on Pine Street?

A: Yes, my house is on Pine Street. (So B continues asking.)

B: Is your roof gray?

A: No, my roof isn't gray. (So it's A's turn to ask a question.)

Exercise 8.   Multiple Choice. Circle the letter of the correct answer.

1. "Is this a new book?"
   "Yes, it is. It's _____ birthday present from John. He gave it to me yesterday."
   (A) his   (C) your
   (B) my   (D) their

2. Sarah is going on a trip to England. She is at the airport. She has _____ passport and suitcase.
   (A) she   (C) her
   (B) she's   (D) with

3. "Do you like the Beatles' music?"
   "No, I don't like _____ music. Do you?"
   (A) their   (C) its
   (B) they   (D) it's

4. "Do you and your husband have a daughter?"
   "Yes, we do. _____ daughter is named Trina, and she lives in Houston."
   (A) Her   (C) She
   (B) Our   (D) We

5. "Oh, excuse me. Am I sitting in _____ seat?"
   "Oh, no. That's not my seat. I'm sitting over there by the door."
   (A) his   (C) your
   (B) my   (D) their

6. Paul and Bob have _____ ID cards with them.
   (A) his   (C) your
   (B) my   (D) their

7. "I'd like to cash this check, please."
   "OK. But I need to see _____ driver's license or some kind of ID."
   (A) his   (C) your
   (B) my   (D) their

8. "Do Mr. and Mrs. Lee have a car?"
   "Yes, they do. _____ is a blue Toyota Corolla."
   (A) They car new   (C) Their new car
   (B) They new car   (D) Their car new

Exercise 9.   Review Test

Part 1.   Underline the correct words.

1. Does Susan like (they, their) new car?   6. (Our, We) class finishes at 9 A.M.

2. That is (his, he) watch.   7. When is (we, our) next meeting?

3. (They, Their) house is gray and white.   8. Tom likes cats. (He, His) pets are all cats.

4. Please show me (your, you) new ring.   9. Tom has a cat. (Its, It) name is Puff.

5. (My, I) know her address.   10. (He, His) exam grade is 83.

Part 2.   Look at the picture. Then read the sentences and write the correct possessive words.

Rachel

I am Rachel Hanks. This is a picture of ___my___ family. The woman on the left is ___my___ grandmother. ___her___ name is Rosa Hanks.

The man on the right is ___my___ uncle. ___his___ name is Ken. The woman near him is ___his___ wife. ___her___ name is Sarah.

Do you see the two kids in the lower right-hand corner of the picture? Those are my cousins. ___their___ names are Zane and Vicky. Can you see ___it's___ cat? It's sitting on the floor. ___it's___ name is Boots.

Of course there are many more people in my family, but they are "camera shy"!

Part 3.   Read each sentence carefully. Look at the underlined part. If the underlined part is correct, circle the word *correct*. If it is wrong, circle the wrong part and write the correct form above.

correct	wrong	1. Karen takes <u>she lunch</u> to school every day.
correct	wrong	2. The man is a doctor. <u>He</u> lives in a very big house.
correct	wrong	3. <u>My telephone number</u> is 222-8884.
correct	wrong	4. Do you like <u>they're new</u> car? It's silver.
correct	wrong	5. Ben and I study hard. <u>Our class</u> is really difficult.
correct	wrong	6. <u>Your</u> answer is very good.
correct	wrong	7. This is <u>my cat. Its name</u> is Fluffy.

Unit 5

Past Tense of *Be*

1. affirmative   2. negative   3. questions   4. short answers

now	**last month**	**last year**

I am in New York now.	**I was in Paris last month.**	**We were in Cairo last year.**

Past Tense of *Be*

Present
I **am** in class now.
You **are** here today.
He **is** hungry now.
She **is** a good swimmer.
It **is** hot today.

We **are** in class.
You **are** American citizens.
They **are** on the table now.

Past
I **was** in class yesterday.
You **were** here yesterday.
He **was** hungry last night.
She **was** a good swimmer.
It **was** hot yesterday.

We **were** in class.
You **were** Vietnamese citizens.
They **were** on the table 5 minutes ago.★

★ **Ago** is used in the past. It tells how far back in the past something happened. Look at the examples on page 61.

60

examples: I arrived here ten minutes ago.
She died one year ago.
I was in New York two months ago.
The war was fifty years ago.

I
he
she   } **was**
it

you
we   } **were**
they

am   becomes   **was**   in the past.
is   becomes   **was**   in the past.   They both end in **s:** i <u>s</u> /w a <u>s</u> .
are becomes   **were** in the past.   They both end in **re:** a <u>r e</u> /w e <u>r e</u> .

Present   *Past*
am   is   are   **was   were**

Negative: was → **was not** OR **wasn't**   were → **were not** OR **weren't**

CAREFUL! Watch out for these common mistakes.

1. Do not use **am, is,** or **are** in past tense sentences.
    wrong: I am born in 1979.
    correct: I was born in 1979.

    wrong: Yesterday it is too hot for me to play tennis.
    correct: Yesterday it was too hot for me to play tennis.

2. Use **was** for **I, he, she,** and **it**; use **were** for **you, we,** and **they.**
    wrong: In 1985, my parents was in India.
    correct: In 1985, my parents were in India.

    wrong: Was you in class this morning?
    correct: Were you in class this morning?

Exercise 1.   Write *was* or *were* on the lines. Follow the example.

example: The little boy ___was___ happy at the party.

1. The weather _____ beautiful yesterday.

2. The best score on the test _____ 97.

3. I _____ at the bank at 4 P.M. yesterday.

4. He _____ in the kitchen 10 minutes ago.

5. Jan and Sue _____ in Japan last year.

6. When I _____ a child, my favorite food _____ spaghetti.

7. Kennedy _____ president from 1960 to 1963.

8. Martina Navratilova _____ the number one tennis player in 1987.

9. You _____ here yesterday.

10. We _____ late to class yesterday.

Exercise 2. In each sentence, there is a difference from the previous sentence. Look at the change. Write the correct form of *be: am, is, are, was, were.*

Beginning sentence: Susan is here now.

1. I   I _____ here now.

2. yesterday   I _____ here yesterday.

3. they   They _____ here yesterday.

4. last week   They _____ here last week.

5. Mr. Lim   Mr. Lim _____ here last week.

6. right now   Mr. Lim _____ here right now.

7. 10 minutes ago   Mr. Lim _____ here 10 minutes ago.

8. I   I _____ here 10 minutes ago.

9. Ashley   Ashley _____ here 10 minutes ago.

10. Ashley and Susan   Ashley and Susan _____ here 10 minutes ago.

11. Susan   Susan _____ here 10 minutes ago.

12. now   Susan _____ here now.

Exercise 3. Read the sentences. Some of the verbs are in the wrong tense. Draw a line through the wrong forms of *be* and change them to the correct forms. Follow the example.

example: *A:* Where is the dictionary?

   B: I don't know where it is now.

   A: It ~~is~~ here on the table yesterday.
   was

   B: I know, but it ~~was~~ not here now.
   is

1. *A:* What is the biggest country in the world now?

   B: I think Russia was the biggest country.

   C: What about the Soviet Union?

   A: The Soviet Union is the biggest country.

   B: Right, from 1918 to 1993, it is the biggest country in the world.

2. *A:* What do you know about Christopher Columbus?

   B: He is from the city of Genoa. He is a famous explorer.

   A: When is he born?

   B: He is born in 1451.

3. *A:* Who were Washington and Lincoln?

   B: That is an easy question. Washington is the first president of the U.S.

   A: And what about Lincoln?

   B: Abraham Lincoln is the sixteenth president. He was the president in the Civil War.

   A: When was Washington born?

   B: He was born in 1732.

   A: What about Lincoln?

   B: In 1809. Lincoln is born ten years after Washington died.

Exercise 4.   **Speaking Activity: Present to Past Drill**

Step 1.   Do student A OR student B. Do *one* of these only.

Step 2.   Number the left lines from 1 to 10 in any order. Mix up the numbers.

Step 3.   Fill in the right lines with *was* or *were*. (Follow the examples.) Check your answers with another student who did the same part (A or B) as you did.

Step 4.   Work with a partner who did not do the same part as you. Student A will read out all ten items as quickly as possible in numerical order. Student B must close the book and listen and then complete the items correctly. For example, student A will say, "Peter is," and student B must say, "Peter was." If this is correct, student A says, "That's correct." If this is not correct, student A says, "Try again," and repeats the item. When all the items are finished, student B will read out the other ten items.

        examples: Melissa is = Melissa ___was___

                   the grammar test is = the grammar test ___was___

Student A	Student B
___. you are = you _____	___. he is = he _____
___. the girl is = the girl _____	___. Rachel is = Rachel _____
___. the cat is = the cat _____	___. the cats are = the cats _____
___. today is = yesterday _____	___. we are = we _____
___. Peter is = Peter _____	___. the shoes are = the shoes _____
___. Joe and Pam are = Joe and Pam _____	___. the teacher is = the teacher _____
___. my car is = my car _____	___. Brazil is = Brazil _____
___. the boys are = the boys _____	___. the boy is = the boy _____
___. dinner is = dinner _____	___. I am = I _____
___. they are = they _____	___. the weather is = the weather _____

Negative

To make a negative statement with **was** or **were,** add the word **not** after **was** or **were.** It is also possible to use contractions (= short forms): **was not** OR **wasn't; were not** OR **weren't.**

Karla was hungry. Peggy **was not** hungry.
I was happy. I **wasn't** sad.
The shirts were cheap. They **weren't** expensive.
Lincoln was the 16th president. He **was not** the 1st president.
He was born in New York. He **wasn't** born in Chicago.

CAREFUL! Watch out for these common mistakes.

1. Do not use **don't** or **doesn't** with **was** and **were.**
    wrong: I don't was here yesterday.
    correct: I wasn't here yesterday.

    wrong: James and Mark don't were late for class.
    correct: James and Mark weren't late for class.

2. Do not say **no was** or **no were.** Say **wasn't (was not)** or **weren't (were not).**
    wrong: The food last night no was good.
    correct: The food last night wasn't good.

    wrong: The apples on the tree no were red.
    correct: The apples on the tree weren't red.

Exercise 5.   Complete the sentences with the correct negatives. Follow the example.

example: Brenda __wasn't__ in Canada last week. She was in Alaska.

1. Lynn _____ a good student when she was in high school.

2. I _____ in class yesterday. My friend said it _____ a very interesting class.

3. The cars _____ very dirty. They were clean.

4. The cat _____ black and white. It was gray.

5. She _____ more than 30 years old when she got married. She was only 25.

6. The test _____ very difficult. All the questions were easy to answer.

7. Basketball is very popular in the U.S., but the inventor of basketball _____ an American. (He was a Canadian.)

8. Henry and I _____ ready for the test. We didn't know many of the answers.

9. Zina _____ the winner of the tennis tournament. She was very upset about this.

10. Mrs. Blackwell _____ my teacher last semester. My teacher was Mrs. Bosley.

Exercise 6.   Speaking Activity: Past Negative Drill (see directions for exercise 4). Fill in the right lines with *wasn't* or *weren't*. Follow the examples.

examples: the books aren't = the books __weren't__
             summer isn't = summer __wasn't__

Student A	Student B
___. lunch isn't = lunch _____	___. I am not = I _____
___. my friends aren't = my friends _____	___. the weather isn't = the weather _____
___. today isn't = yesterday _____	___. we aren't = we _____
___. Peter isn't = Peter _____	___. my shoes aren't = my shoes _____

___. you aren't = you _____   ___. he isn't = he _____

___. the child isn't = the child _____   ___. Andy isn't = Andy _____

___. the cat isn't = the cat _____   ___. Japan isn't = Japan _____

___. my parents aren't = my   ___. my brother isn't = my brother _____

parents _____

___. Ben and Ted aren't = Ben and   ___. the teacher isn't = the teacher _____

Ted _____

___. the birds aren't = the birds _____   ___. my car isn't = my car _____

Homework suggestion: Have students write complete TRUE sentences using any of the above structures.

examples: Lunch wasn't delicious yesterday.
I wasn't in Mexico last week.

Making a Question

To make a *yes-no* question, move **was** or **were** to the beginning:

Statement	*Question*
Mark was in the kitchen.	Was Mark in the kitchen?
Leo was late to class on Monday.	Was Leo late to class on Monday?
The shoes were $60.	Were the shoes $60?
You were tired after the game.	Were you tired after the game?

CAREFUL! Watch out for these common mistakes.

1. Do not begin a **was/were** question with **do, does,** or **did.**
   wrong: Did you were born in 1980?
   correct: Were you born in 1980?

   wrong: Does the weather yesterday was very hot?
   correct: Was the weather yesterday very hot?

2. In writing, do not forget to begin **was/were** questions with **was** or **were.**
   wrong: You were hungry? (OK in speaking)
   correct: Were you hungry?

   wrong: The book was very expensive? (OK in speaking)
   correct: Was the book very expensive?

Exercise 7.   Read each statement and then make a question using the word
yesterday. Follow the examples.

Step 1.   First, do this by yourself as homework.
Step 2.   Then, check your questions with a partner in class. One student reads the
present tense sentence from the book, and the other student has to say
the past tense question. Only one student should look at the book.

examples: George is tired today. _Was George tired yesterday?_
             They are hungry now. _Were they hungry yesterday?_

1. Mrs. Smith is happy today. _____

2. The cats are thirsty now. _____

3. Paul and Naomi are in class today. _____

4. The weather is cold now. _____

5. His homework is correct. _____

6. You are late to class today. _____

7. The kitchen is dirty today. _____

8. The store is open now. _____

9. The park is crowded today. _____

10. Sam and Vick are sleepy today. _____

11. The teacher is busy now. _____

12. Robert is early today. _____

Exercise 8.   Make nine *yes-no* questions from the information. Sometimes
more than one answer is possible. Follow the example.

the teacher	the kittens	your dinner
the movie	Sandra and Kevin	the weather
the baby	her parents	the flight from Vancouver

1. tired after class

    Was the teacher tired after class?

2. really hot

    _____

3. late by 15 minutes

    _____

4. better than the book

_____

5. delicious

_____

6. born at General Hospital

_____

7. in the same class last year

_____

8. students at the same high school

_____

9. hungry

_____

Short Answers

To answer a *yes-no* question, use **was, wasn't, were,** or **weren't** in your answer.

question:	Were you sleepy last night?
full answer:	Yes, I was sleepy last night. No, I wasn't sleepy last night.
short answer:	Yes, I was. No, I wasn't.
question:	Were the apples fresh?
full answer:	Yes, the apples were fresh. No, the apples weren't fresh.
short answer:	Yes, they were. No, they weren't.

CAREFUL! Watch out for this common mistake.

Do not use **do/does/did** as a short answer for **was/were** questions.
   wrong: Was Nancy home last night? Yes, she did.
   correct: Was Nancy home last night? Yes, she was.

wrong: Were the students happy after the test? No, they don't.
correct: Were the students happy after the test? No, they weren't.

Exercise 9.   Write the two possible short answers for each question. Follow the
                 example.

                 example: Was the test easy?
                              <u>   Yes, it was   </u>. OR <u>   No, it wasn't   </u>.

   1. Was the party at John's house fun?

       _____. OR _____.

   2. Were Sam, Mark, and Ron in the same class last year?

       _____. OR _____.

   3. Were you sleepy in class yesterday?

       _____. OR _____.

   4. Was the food at the dinner party delicious?

       _____. OR _____.

   5. Were you and Gina on the same team in the volleyball match?

       _____. OR _____.

   6. Was the Soviet Union the biggest country in the world in 1980?

       _____. OR _____.

   7. Was the teacher the first person in the class today?

       _____. OR _____.

   8. Were the Chinese people the first to use gunpowder?

       _____. OR _____.

   9. Was the homework difficult?

       _____. OR _____.

  10. Was Mary in the kitchen?

       _____. OR _____.

Exercise 10.   Speaking Activity. Interview a student in your class. Choose five of the questions from below. Write the questions on the lines before you do the interview. Make a prediction about how many *yes* answers your partner will give to your questions.

Student's name: _____   Prediction YES _____ / Actual YES: ____

Question 1: _____

Answer: Your prediction: _____   His/Her real answer: _____

Question 2: _____

Answer: Your prediction: _____   His/Her real answer: _____

Question 3: _____

Answer: Your prediction: _____   His/Her real answer: _____

Question 4: _____

Answer: Your prediction: _____   His/Her real answer: _____

Question 5: _____

Answer: Your prediction: _____   His/Her real answer: _____

Questions: Were you a quiet baby?
Were you a good student in elementary school?
Was your favorite color green when you were a child?
Were you born in a hospital?
Were you born on a weekend?
Was the TV on last night when you went to sleep?
Was your first pet a cat?
Were you good at math in school?
Were you the firstborn in your family?
Was collecting stamps one of your hobbies when you were a child?

More practice: Do this exercise again with another student. Use some of the same questions or make your own original questions. Practice using *was* and *were*.

Exercise 11.   Multiple Choice. Circle the letter of the correct answer.

1. "Was the movie good?"

    "_____. I enjoyed it very much."

    (A) No, it wasn't.   (C) No, I wasn't.

    (B) Yes, it was.   (D) Yes, I was.

2. The name on all of the books _____ "Mary D. Smith."

   (A) was   (C) were

   (B) it was   (D) they were

3. "I'm so tired today."

   "_____ tired yesterday, too?"

   (A) Was I   (C) Am I

   (B) Were you   (D) Are you

4. "Was Paul Johnson in math class yesterday?"

   "I'm not sure, but I think he _____ there."

   (A) is   (C) in class

   (B) was   (D) yesterday

5. "_____ at Linda's house fun?"

   "Yes, it was. We had a good time there."

   (A) The party was   (C) Was the party

   (B) The people were   (D) Were the people

6. "Was the trip very long?"

   "Yes, it was. _____."

   (A) The driver was tired.   (C) The tired driver was.

   (B) Was tired the driver?   (D) Tired was the driver?

7. "How was the beach yesterday?"

   "Wonderful. It wasn't very hot, and the water _____ very clear."

   (A) are   (C) is

   (B) were   (D) was

8. "Were all the answers on your test correct?"

   "No, _____. Number 7 was wrong."

   (A) they weren't   (C) they aren't

   (B) it wasn't   (D) it isn't

Exercise 12.   Review Test

Part 1.   Read this short passage. Fill in each blank with any word that makes sense.

Joe and I went to see a movie last night. We both liked the movie very much. Joe

_____ very happy because our tickets _____ not expensive! A ticket at that

theater is usually $7 for one person, but last night a ticket _____ only $3.   The

movie _____ very good. The main actor died at the end of this movie, so I

_____ very sad.

Part 2.   Read this short passage. There are five mistakes. Circle the mistakes and write the correct form above the mistake.

When I am a little boy, my best pet was a cat. My cat's name is Sammy. Sammy was a

beautiful cat. His face was white, and his ears are black. His body is black and white.

Sammy liked to play outside. He is a really good pet. I have a picture of Sammy in my

photo album. This picture was taken in 1974. That was over twenty years ago.

Part 3.   Read each sentence carefully. Look at the underlined part. If the underlined part is correct, circle the word *correct.* If it is wrong, circle the wrong part and write the correct form above.

correct   wrong   1. The Soviet Union <u>was</u> a very big country.

correct   wrong   2. After I finished my homework last night, I <u>am</u> very tired.

correct   wrong   3. Today it is very hot, but yesterday it <u>is</u> not so hot.

correct   wrong   4. Kennedy and Nixon <u>was</u> presidents of the United States.

correct   wrong   5. My great-grandparents <u>were</u> from Italy.

correct   wrong   6. People say that the cost of living in New York City <u>is</u> expensive.

correct   wrong   7. In 1945, the U.N. <u>was</u> not very big. Now there are many members.

Unit 6

Past Tense of Regular and Irregular Verbs

Regular verbs: 1. affirmative   3. negative   4. questions
                     2. spelling of *ed* (double letter or not) 5. short answers

Irregular verbs: 1. affirmative   2. negative   3. questions

What did *Joe* and *Mark* do yesterday?

Joe	Mark

Joe washed his car.
wash – washed

Mark did his homework.
do – did

Joe listened to music.
listen – listened

Mark ate ice cream.
eat – ate

Joe watched TV.
watch – watched

Mark wrote a letter.
write – wrote

VERB + *ed*

VERB + ?

Discover Grammar

1. Look at the box below. Circle all the verbs on the left side of the box and on the right side of the box.

    There are two differences between the verbs on the left side and the verbs on the right side.

2. What is different about the verbs? _____

    _____

3. What is different about the times of the sentences? _____

    _____

[Check page 92 for answers to these questions.]

Past Tense of Verbs

Present	*Past*
I live in an apartment.	I lived in an apartment last year.
You walk to class every day.	You walked to class yesterday.
He usually works in the day.	He worked last night.
She studies English here.	She studied French in France in 1994.
It rains a lot in the summer.	It rained a lot yesterday.
We sometimes talk about our problems.	We talked about our problems last night.
They arrive late sometimes.	They arrived late this morning.

Now look at these examples.

	WORK	**LIVE**	**STUDY**	**WANT**	**NEED**
I	I worked	I lived	I studied	I wanted	I needed
you	you worked	you lived	you studied	you wanted	you needed
he	he worked	he lived	he studied	he wanted	he needed
she	she worked	she lived	she studied	she wanted	she needed
it	it worked	it lived	it studied	it wanted	it needed
we	we worked	we lived	we studied	we wanted	we needed
they	they worked	they lived	they studied	they wanted	they needed
		e — (+d)	y—i (+ed)		

In present tense, a verb has one form: **VERB + ed.**
This is different from the present tense. Present tense has two forms (**VERB** or **VERB + s**).

CAREFUL! Watch out for these common mistakes.

1. Don't use **VERB** or **VERB** + **s** in the past tense. Don't forget to use **ed.**
   wrong: Laura cooks scrambled eggs for breakfast yesterday.
   correct: Laura cooked scrambled eggs for breakfast yesterday.

   wrong: Emily study French last year.
   correct: Emily studied French last year.

2. Do not use **was/were** with verbs in simple past tense.
   wrong: I was walk to school yesterday.
   correct: I walked to school yesterday.

   wrong: He was study last night.
   correct: He studied last night.

3. Don't forget to change **y** to **i** and add **ed.**★
   wrong: My baby sister cryed last night.
   correct: My baby sister cried last night.

4. If a verb ends in **consonant-vowel-consonant (C-V-C),** don't forget to double the last consonant before adding **ed.**
   wrong: He stoped the tape.
   correct: He stopped the tape. (stop: t = C, o = V, p = C)

   wrong: Two masked men robed the bank!
   correct: Two masked men robbed the bank! (rob: r = C, o = V, b = C)

   wrong: Maria cleanned her jewelry.
   correct: Maria cleaned her jewelry. (clean: e = V, a = V, n = C)

   ★We don't change **y** to **i** if the letter before **y** is a vowel **(a,e,i,o,u).**
   examples: play, played; enjoy, enjoyed; but try, tried; study, studied

---

Exercise 1.   Write the forms of *work* in present and past tenses. Follow the examples.

Present

1. I __work__ every day.
2. You __work__ at night.
3. He __works__ all of the time.
4. She __works__ every day.
5. It __works__ most of the time.
6. We __work__ every afternoon.
7. They __work__ here every day.

Past

8. I __worked__ yesterday.
9. You __worked__ last night.
10. He __worked__ an hour ago.
11. She __worked__ yesterday.
12. It __worked__ last week.
13. We __worked__ in 1993.
14. They __worked__ here yesterday.

15. Make a list of the time expressions used in the left column. These are time expressions that we can use with simple present tense: _____

_____.

16. Make a list of the time expressions used in the right column. These are time expressions that we can use with simple past tense:

_____

_____.

Exercise 2. Fill in the blanks with the correct past tense forms of the verbs. Follow the examples.

LEARN
I _learned_
you _learned_
she _learned_
it _learned_
we _learned_
they _learned_

LIKE
I _liked_
you _liked_
she _liked_
it _liked_
we _liked_
they _liked_

WATCH
I _watched_
you _watched_
she _watched_
it _watched_
we _watched_
they _watched_

WASH
I _washed_
you _washed_
she _washed_
it _washed_
we _washed_
they _washed_

CHOP
I _chopped_
you _chopped_
he _chopped_
we _chopped_
you _chopped_
Jo and Sue _chopped_

WATCH
I _watched_
you _watched_
he _watched_
we _watched_
you _watched_
Jo and Sue _watched_

PRACTICE
I _practiced_
you _practiced_
he _practiced_
we _practiced_
you _practiced_
Jo and Sue _practiced_

TRY
I _tried_
you _tried_
he _tried_
we _tried_
you _tried_
Jo and Sue _tried_

STUDY
I _studied_
you _studied_

LISTEN
I _listened_
you _listened_

PLAY
I _played_
you _played_

REPEAT
I _repeated_
you _repeated_

we _studied_	we _listened_	we _played_	we _repeated_
they _studied_	they _listened_	they _played_	they _repeated_
Sue _studied_	Sue _listened_	Sue _played_	Sue _repeated_

Exercise 3.   Write the past tense forms of the verbs. Follow the example.

1. I want   _I wanted_
2. they attend   _they atended_
3. you repeat   _you repeated_
4. we talk   _we talked_
5. we need   _we needed_
6. it repeats   _it repeated_
7. I count   _I counted_
8. they type   _they typed_
9. I watch   _I watched_
10. you shout   _you shouted_

11. she listens   _she listened_
12. I wait   _I waited_
13. he learns   _he learned_
14. they explain   _thy explained_
15. she uses   _she used_
16. you like   _you liked_
17. she adds   _she added_
18. I shop   _I shoped_
19. we study   _we studied_
20. he answers   _he answered_

Pronunciation Problem: *ed*

There are three ways to pronounce the letters in past tense.

1. /t/ if the last sound of the verb is **k, p, s, ch, sh, f**
   ki<u>ck</u>ed, hel<u>p</u>ed, mi<u>ss</u>ed, wat<u>ch</u>ed, wa<u>sh</u>ed, lau<u>gh</u>ed (*gh = f*)

2. /d/ if the last sound of the verb is **g, b, z, ge, v,** vowel
   be<u>gg</u>ed, ro<u>bb</u>ed, plea<u>s</u>ed (se = <u>z</u>), pa<u>g</u>ed, li<u>v</u>ed, pla<u>y</u>ed, sa<u>w</u>ed

3. /ɪd/ if the last sound is **d, t**
   nee<u>d</u>ed, wan<u>t</u>ed

IMPORTANT: Remember that the last **sound** is important, **not** the last **letter.**

example 1: **bake**   The last letter is **e,** but the last sound is **k.**
                   baked: the **ed** sounds like /t/

example 2: **laugh**   The last letter is **h,** but the last sound is **f.**
                   laughed: the **ed** sounds like /t/

Exercise 4.   How do you pronounce these verbs in the past tense? Circle the one verb in each group that is different. Follow the examples.

     examples: repeated   talked   added
             (The answer is *talked* because it ends in /t/ but *repeated* and *added* end in /ɪd/.)

              answered   kissed   arrived
             (The answer is *kissed* because it ends in /t/ but *answered* and *arrived* end in /d/.)

1. walked	visited	added		6. coughed	shaved	remembered
2. wanted	listened	attended		7. rained	folded	studied
3. cooked	erased	cleaned		8. liked	shopped	presented
4. repeated	answered	attended		9. smiled	explained	introduced
5. ironed	used	needed		10. shouted	snowed	signed

Exercise 5.   Say the past tense of each verb. There are five verbs with /t/, six verbs with /d/, and four verbs with /ɪd/.

Step 1.   Circle the sound of the letters *ed*.
Step 2.   Then use these words to finish the sentences.

(A) robbed	t d ɪd	(F) failed	t d ɪd	(K) signed	t d ɪd
(B) waited	t d ɪd	(G) sneezed	t d ɪd	(L) cooked	t d ɪd
(C) needed	t d ɪd	(H) counted	t d ɪd	(M) carried	t d ɪd
(D) erased	t d ɪd	(I) passed	t d ɪd	(N) helped	t d ɪd
(E) washed	t d ɪd	(J) ironed	t d ɪd	(O) folded	t d ɪd

1. John's answer was wrong, so he _____ it.

2. A man with a mask _____ the bank yesterday.

3. Barbara _____, and Jill said "Bless you."

4. I _____ my name at the bottom of the check.

5. Robert _____ steak and potatoes for dinner last night.

6. The clothes were dirty, so I _____ them. After that, I _____
    the pants and I _____ the short pants, towels, and underwear.

7. The books were very heavy, so I only _____ half of them.

8. The math homework was difficult, but Susan _____ me with it.

9. I walked to the store because I _____ some bread.

10. John _____ the grammar test. His score was only 45.

11. Tim _____ the reading test. His score was 93.

12. Yesterday we _____ for the bus for one hour!

13. The teacher _____ all the books. There were 27 books.

Exercise 6.   Present and Past Tenses of Verbs. Underline the correct verb tense. Read the time expressions carefully. Follow the examples.

1. Mr. Smith (play, <u>plays</u>, played) tennis every morning. Yesterday it (rain, rains, <u>rained</u>) in the morning, so he (play, plays, played) in the late afternoon. At that time, the tennis court (is, was) dry.

2. Now it (is, was) 9 A.M. The supermarket (open, opens, opened) an hour ago.

3. Cats (like, likes, liked) fish very much. My cat (love, loves, loved) fish for dinner.

4. Mrs. Keats is a good cook. I really (like, likes, liked) her food. She sometimes (try, tries, tried) new kinds of food. Last night she (cook, cooks, cooked) fish with lime. It (is, was) delicious. That (is, was) my first time to eat fish with lime.

5. Yesterday morning I was very busy. I (clean, cleans, cleaned) the house from 8 to 9. Then I (wash, washes, washed) my car. Then I (plant, plants, planted) some flowers in my garden. Finally, I (play, plays, played) tennis. It was a really busy morning.

6. Sometimes my parents (call, calls, called) me late at night. For example, they (call, calls, called) me at 11 P.M. last night.

7. Mary and Sue (work, works, worked) in the same office. Mary (work, works, worked) in the morning, and Sue (work, works, worked) in the afternoon. They (work, worked) from Monday to Friday.

8. Ian usually (play, plays, played) hockey with his friends on Saturday morning. However, last Saturday it was too cold. He (watch, watches, watched) a hockey game on TV instead.

Exercise 7.   Write any correct verb in each blank. Use the correct verb tenses. You will use some verbs more than once. Check your answers with a partner.

arrive	clean	want	call	study
explain	ask	answer	be	walk
finish	watch	cook	start	wash

1. I _____ TV last night with my friend James. James

    _____ at my house at 7:15. We _____ a program

    about tennis. The program _____ at 7:30. It _____

    at 8:30.

2. Emily and Susan _____ dinner last night for ten people. It

    _____ a special dinner. After the dinner, Bob and I

    _____ the dishes. George and Emma _____ the

    kitchen area.

3. I _____ to study with Bob last night, so I _____ him.

    I _____ him about his plans for the evening. He also

    _____ to study with me, so I _____ from my house

    to Bob's house. We _____ from 7 to 10.

4. The teacher _____ the new grammar lesson to us. Two students

    _____ a question, and the teacher _____ their

    questions.

Past Tense of Verbs: Negative

Affirmative	*Negative*
I **liked** the movie.	I **did not like** the movie.
You **practiced** the verbs.	You **didn't practice** the verbs.
He **called** Jennifer.	He **did not call** Jennifer.
She **needed** a dollar.	She **did not need** a dollar.
It **rained** hard last night.	It **didn't rain** hard last night.
We **introduced** Bob to Jim.	We **did not introduce** Bob to Jim.
They **walked** to the store.	They **did not walk** to the store.

Grammar

To make a negative statement with a *past tense verb,* add **did not** before **VERB.**

It is also possible to use contractions (= short forms): *did not* OR *didn't.*

| I you he she it we they | + | did not (didn't) | + | VERB |

In past tense, a verb has one negative form: **did not (didn't).**

CAREFUL! Watch out for these common mistakes.

1. Do not forget to use **didn't.**
   wrong: Katie not study French last night.
   correct: Katie did not study French last night. (OR didn't)

   wrong: The U.S. no start with 100 states.
   correct: The U.S. didn't start with 100 states. (OR did not)

2. Do not use **wasn't,** or **weren't** with **VERB.** Use **didn't** only.
   wrong: The man wasn't like the food at the party.
   correct: The man didn't like the food at the party. (OR did not)

   wrong: Nell and Vick weren't play tennis yesterday.
   correct: Nell and Vick didn't play tennis yesterday. (OR did not)

3. Do not use *ed* in the negative. **Did** is past, and you only need a past tense part in one place in the verb.
   wrong: I didn't studied last night.
   correct: I didn't study last night.

   wrong: The dinner didn't started at 7 P.M.
   correct: The dinner didn't start at 7 P.M.

Exercise 8.   Fill in the blanks with the correct forms of the verbs.

	Present	Present Negative	Past	Past Negative
1. I/want	I want	I don't want	I wanted	I didn't want
2. he/listen	He listens	He doesn't listen	He listened	He didn't listens
3. they/learn	They learn	They don't learn	They learned	They didn't learn
4. Bill/like	Bill likes	Bill doesn't like	Bill liked	Bill didn't like
5. we/watch	we watch	we don't watch	we watched	we didn't watch
6. you/practice	you practice	you don't practice	you practiced	you did'n practice
7. he/study	he studies	he doesn't study	he studied	he didn't study
8. I/play	I play	I don't play	I played	I didn't play
9. it/repeat	It repeats	It doesn't repeat	It repeated	It didn't repeat
10. they/shop	they shop	they don't shop	they shopped	they didn't shop
11. we/mail	we mail	we don't mail	we mailed	we didn't mail
12. he/explain	he explains	he doesn't explain	he explained	he doesn't explain
13. I/answer	I answer	I don't answer	I answered	I didn't answer
14. she/chop	She chops	she doesn't chop	she chopped	she didn't chop
15. we/erase	we erase	we don't	we erased	we didn't erase

Exercise 9. Write ten negative sentences in the past about yourself. Make six of the sentences TRUE and four of the sentences FALSE. Use a different verb in each sentence. Circle T if your sentence is true and F if it is false. Then work with a partner. Read your sentence and see if your partner can guess if a sentence is TRUE or FALSE. Who can guess more correct answers?

example: T   F   ___I didn't study last year.___
             T   F   ___My brother didn't call me last week.___

1. T   F   _____
2. T   F   _____
3. T   F   _____
4. T   F   _____
5. T   F   _____
6. T   F   _____
7. T   F   _____
8. T   F   _____
9. T   F   _____
10. T   F   _____

(*After you finish:* Are there any surprises? Are there any interesting facts?)

Making a Question

A *yes-no* question for a simple past tense verb begins with **did**:

Statement	Question
I arrived after you.	Did I arrive after you?
You played hockey last week.	Did you play hockey last week?
He worked in Mexico one year.	Did he work in Mexico one year?
She studied Chinese in college.	Did she study Chinese in college?
It snowed last month.	Did it snow last month?
We washed all the dishes.	Did we wash all the dishes?
They lived in Italy in 1985.	Did they live in Italy in 1985?

CAREFUL! Watch out for these common mistakes.

1. Don't forget to use **did.**

   | wrong: | Talked John to you last night? |
   | correct: | Did John talk to you last night? |

   | wrong: | You studied English? |
   | correct: | Did you study English? |

2. Do not put **ed** or **s** on the verb in *yes-no* questions. Use only the base (simple) form of the verb.

   | wrong: | Did Valerie walked to the bank? |
   | correct: | Did Valerie walk to the bank? |

   | wrong: | Did the car uses 10 gallons of gas last week? |
   | correct: | Did the car use 10 gallons of gas last week? |

3. Do not begin past tense verb questions with **was** or **were.**

   | wrong: | Was he call you last night? |
   | correct: | Did he call you last night? |

   | wrong: | Were Harry and Emily shopped together yesterday? |
   | correct: | Did Harry and Emily shop together yesterday? |

Exercise 10.   Underline the correct word. Follow the example.

example: (Were, <u>Did</u>) Fred and Tim live in the same apartment last year?

1. (Was, Did) you work yesterday?

2. Did John (wait, waits, waited) for you after the movie?

3. (Were, Did) it rain a lot last night?

4. Did the waiter (counted, count, counts) all the coins correctly?

5. Did you (uses, use, used) a pencil on the test yesterday?

6. (Did, Does) she study last night?

7. Did I (snore, snores, snored) last night?

8. Did Mr. Miller (present, presented, presents) lesson 8 last week?

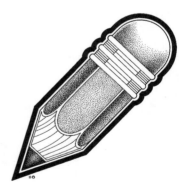

Exercise 11.   Read these conversations. Write the correct words on the lines. Follow the examples.

(finish)   *Bob:*   <u>Did</u>   Mary <u>finish</u>   the homework last night?

              Sue: No, <u>she didn't finish</u> the homework last night.

                     <u>She finished</u>   the homework at 6 this morning.

(want)   *Ann:*   <u>Does</u>   Luke <u>want</u>   coffee with cream?

              Tim: No, <u>he doesn't want</u>   coffee with cream.

                     Yolanda <u>wants</u>   coffee with cream.

1.   (dream)★   *Tim:*   _____ you _____ that you were on a small island in the ocean?

              Sue: No, _____ that I was on a small island in the ocean.

                   _____ that I was at the top of a mountain.

              Tim: Really? That sounds interesting. Tell me more.

2.   (fail)   *Ken:*   She looks sad. _____ she _____ the grammar test?

           Marc: No, _____ the grammar test.

                   _____ the reading test.

           Ken: That's too bad. She studies a lot, but she doesn't do well on tests.

3.   (visit)   *Jeff:*   _____ he _____ his parents last Monday?

            Ann: No, _____ his parents last Monday.

                   _____ his parents last Sunday.

           Jeff: Oh, my mistake. . . . It was Sunday, not Monday.

4.   (laugh)   *Ben:*   _____ you _____ at Brian's joke?

            Sue: No, _____ at Brian's joke.

                   Emily _____ at Brian's joke.

           Ben: I didn't think that Brian's joke was funny.

5.   (lock)   *Hank:*   _____ Mr. Wilson _____ the door?

           Karl: No, _____ the door.

                   Mrs. Wilson _____ the door.

          Hank: Are you sure?

          Karl: Yes, I am. Why?

★*Dream* has two past tense forms: *dreamed, dreamt.*

Short Answers

To answer a *yes-no* question, use **didn't** in your answer.

question:	Did you study Chinese 3 years ago?
full answer:	Yes, I studied Chinese 3 years ago.
	No, I didn't study Chinese 3 years ago.
short answer:	Yes, I did.
	No, I didn't.
question:	Did Emily attend class?
full answer:	Yes, Emily attended class.
	No, Emily didn't attend class.
short answer:	Yes, she did.
	No, she didn't.

CAREFUL! Watch out for this common mistake.

Do not use **was/were** as a short answer for **did** questions.
wrong:	Did Nancy arrive late? Yes, she was.
correct:	Did Nancy arrive late? Yes, she did.
wrong:	Did Jan and Mike travel to Switzerland? No, they weren't.
correct:	Did Jan and Mike travel to Switzerland? No, they didn't.

Exercise 12.   Write the two possible short answers for each question. Follow the example.

example: Did Keith play tennis yesterday?
   <u> Yes, he did </u>. OR <u> No, he didn't </u>.

1. Did you watch TV last night?

    _____. OR _____.

2. Did it rain this morning?

    _____. OR _____.

3. Did the students attend all the classes?

    _____. OR _____.

4. Did you and Ben cook spaghetti last week?

    _____. OR _____.

5. Did the food taste salty?

    _____. OR _____.

Exercise 13.   Speaking Activity: What did you do yesterday? There are twelve activities below. Put a check mark (√) by any five of the activities. Do this in the left "Your Schedule" column. Next, work with a partner. Do NOT show your book to your partner. Take turns asking each other questions. Say "yesterday" in every question. Use complete short answers in your answers. For example, say, "Yes, I did" or "No, I didn't" instead of only "Yes" or "No." If the answer is YES, then you continue. If the answer is NO, then it is your partner's turn. Follow the example.

     example: *A:* Did you study math yesterday?
                     B: No, I didn't. (The answer is NO, so it is B's turn.)
                     B: Did you cook lunch yesterday?
                     A: Yes, I did. (The answer is YES, so B asks again.)

The winner is the student who can guess all five of his or her partner's answers.

Your Schedule	*Your Partner's Schedule*
____ wash the dishes	____ wash the dishes
____ clean the windows	____ clean the windows
____ call your friend	____ call your friend
____ cook lunch	____ cook lunch
____ watch the news on TV	____ watch the news on TV
____ listen to the radio	____ listen to the radio
____ study math	____ study math
____ study English	____ study English
____ ask the teacher a question	____ ask the teacher a question
____ stay awake late	____ stay awake late
____ visit your friend	____ visit your friend
____ play tennis	____ play tennis

List of Irregular Past Tense Verbs★

Most English verbs use **ed** in the past tense: **learned, studied, played.** However, there are some verbs in English that do not use **ed.** The past tense for these verbs is different. Look at these 33 irregular past tense forms.

Present	Past	Present	Past	Present	Past
begin	began	go	went	send	sent
bring	brought	have	had	sleep	slept
buy	bought	hear	heard	speak	spoke
choose	chose	leave	left	spend	spent
come	came	lose	lost	stand	stood
do	did	make	made	take	took
drink	drank	put	put	tell	told
eat	ate	read	read	think	thought
forget	forgot	say	said	understand	understood
get	got	see	saw	wake	woke
give	gave	sell	sold	write	wrote

★There is a longer list on page 186 in the back of the book.

Affirmative Statement	*Negative Statement*★
	subject* + did not (didn't) + *simple verb
I **went** to the park.	I **didn't go** to the store.
You **went** to Miami.	You **did not go** to New York.
He **went** to school.	He **didn't go** to the bank.
She **went** to France.	She **didn't go** to Italy.
The plane **went** to Mexico.	It **didn't go** to Colombia.
We **went** to the store.	We **did not go** home.
They **went** to China.	They **didn't go** to Japan.

Affirmative Statement	*Question Statement*★
	did + *subject* + *simple verb*
I **slept** ten hours.	**Did** I really **sleep** ten hours?
You **ate** all the cheese.	**Did** you **eat** all the cheese?
He **spoke** to Dr. Karl.	**Did** he **speak** to Dr. Karl?
She **came** to the bank at noon.	**Did** she **come** to the bank at noon?
It **took** 1 hour to do the work.	**Did** it **take** 1 hour to do the work?
We **wrote** a letter to Bob.	**Did** we **write** a letter to Bob?
They **brought** a lot of cassettes.	**Did** they **bring** a lot of cassettes?

★Negative and question forms for regular and irregular verbs are the same.

CAREFUL! Watch out for these common mistakes.

1. Do not use **ed** with irregular verbs.
   wrong: My sister goed to England last year.
   correct: My sister went to England last year.

   wrong: He maked a cheese sandwich for lunch.
   correct: He made a cheese sandwich for lunch.

2. Do not use the irregular past tense form with **did** in the question. **Did** is past, and
   you only need a past tense form in one place in the verb.
   wrong: Did you gave the money to John? (= 2 past tense words)
   correct: Did you give the money to John?

   wrong: Did they drank all the juice? (= 2 past tense words)
   correct: Did they drink all the juice?

3. Do not use the irregular past tense form in a negative. **Didn't (did not)** is past,
   and you only need a past tense form in one place in the verb.
   wrong: She didn't understood the lesson. (= 2 past tense words)
   correct: She didn't understand the lesson.

   wrong: Sammy did not took the test yesterday. (= 2 past tense words)
   correct: Sammy did not take the test yesterday.

Exercise 14.   Write the past tense of the verbs on the lines. Follow the examples.

examples: think _thought_   leave _left_

1. drink _____		11. send _____	
2. give _____		12. eat _____	
3. tell _____		13. have _____	
4. read _____		14. make _____	
5. begin _____		15. speak _____	
6. get _____		16. forget _____	
7. see _____		17. put _____	
8. buy _____		18. come _____	
9. take _____		19. write _____	
10. go _____		20. choose _____	

Exercise 15. Make a test for a classmate. What are twenty of the most difficult verbs? Write the present tense of twenty verbs on the left lines. Then give your book to a classmate. The classmate should write the correct past tense. Check your partner's answers.

Present	Past		Present	Past
1. _____ _____		11. _____ _____		
2. _____ _____		12. _____ _____		
3. _____ _____		13. _____ _____		
4. _____ _____		14. _____ _____		
5. _____ _____		15. _____ _____		
6. _____ _____		16. _____ _____		
7. _____ _____		17. _____ _____		
8. _____ _____		18. _____ _____		
9. _____ _____		19. _____ _____		
10. _____ _____		20. _____ _____		

Exercise 16. Write the correct forms of the verbs on the lines. There are regular and irregular verbs in this exercise.

Statement		Negative		Question	
Present	Past	Present	Past	Present	Past
he goes	he went	he doesn't go	he didn't go	Does he go	Did he go
they work	they worked	they don't work	they didn't work	Do they work	Did they work
_____	we began	_____	_____	_____	_____
_____	_____	_____	she didn't get	_____	_____
_____	_____	I don't wake	_____	_____	_____
_____	_____	_____	_____	Do you sell	_____
_____	_____	_____	_____	_____	Did you think
it takes	_____	_____	_____	_____	_____
_____	he spoke	_____	_____	_____	_____
_____	_____	_____	_____	Do I make	_____
_____	_____	_____	he didn't have	_____	_____
_____	_____	_____	she didn't put	_____	_____

Exercise 17.   Write the correct forms of the verbs on the lines. Follow the example.

example: (tell) I __*told*__ the good news to him last night.

1. (give)   She _____ me a check a few minutes ago.

2. (come)   Did you _____ late?

3. (take)   I _____ my medicine over an hour ago.

4. (forget)   He didn't _____ the telephone number.

5. (leave)   Who _____ the party first?

6. (be)   Mark and I _____ in Saudi Arabia for one year.

7. (begin)   The class _____ ten minutes ago.

8. (do)   He didn't _____ the work yesterday.

9. (eat)   We _____ steak last night.

10. (get)   Did Martha _____ sick yesterday?

Exercise 18.   Speaking Activity: What did you do yesterday? There are twelve activities below. Put a check mark (√) by any five of the activities. Do this in the left "Your Schedule" column. Next, work with a partner. Do NOT show your book to your partner. Take turns asking each other questions. Say "yesterday" in every question. If the answer is YES, then you continue. If the answer is NO, then it is your partner's turn. *Use complete sentences in your answers.* Follow the example.

example: A: Did you come to class late yesterday?
           B: No, I didn't come to class late. (The answer is NO, so it is B's turn.)
           B: Did you eat salad yesterday?
           A: Yes, I ate salad yesterday. (The answer is YES, so B asks again.)

The winner is the student who can guess all five of his or her partner's answers.

Your Schedule   *Your Partner's Schedule*

___ wake up at 7 A.M.   ___ wake up at 8 A.M.

___ take a shower in the morning   ___ take a bath in the morning

___ eat toast for breakfast   ___ eat eggs for breakfast

___ drink coffee without sugar   ___ speak Spanish

___ speak Arabic   ___ have a headache

___ write a letter to your friend   ___ speak to your teacher

___ sleep in the afternoon   ___ buy a cheese sandwich

___ find any money in the street   ___ read a newspaper

___ have a headache   ___ drink apple juice

___ spend more than $5   ___ spend more than $10

___ lose your watch   ___ get a letter from your friend

___ see a black cat   ___ come to class late

Answers to DISCOVER GRAMMAR from page 74:

1. (left) live, walk, works, studies, rains, talk, arrive; (right) lived, walked, worked, studied, rained, talked, arrived
2. The verbs on the right end in *ed*.
3. The verbs on the right are all in past tense. These actions happened last year, yesterday, etc.

Exercise 19.   Speaking Activity: The Shopping Bag Game. Look at the shopping bags on page 93. Work with a partner. Each partner chooses one of the sixteen shopping bags. Take turns asking *yes-no* questions to find out which bag is your partner's bag. If student B's answer is YES, student A may continue asking questions. If the answer is NO, then student B asks questions. The first student to guess the price of his or her partner's shopping bag is the winner. Use "Did you buy _____?" and "Yes, I bought _____" or "No, I didn't buy _____" in your conversations.

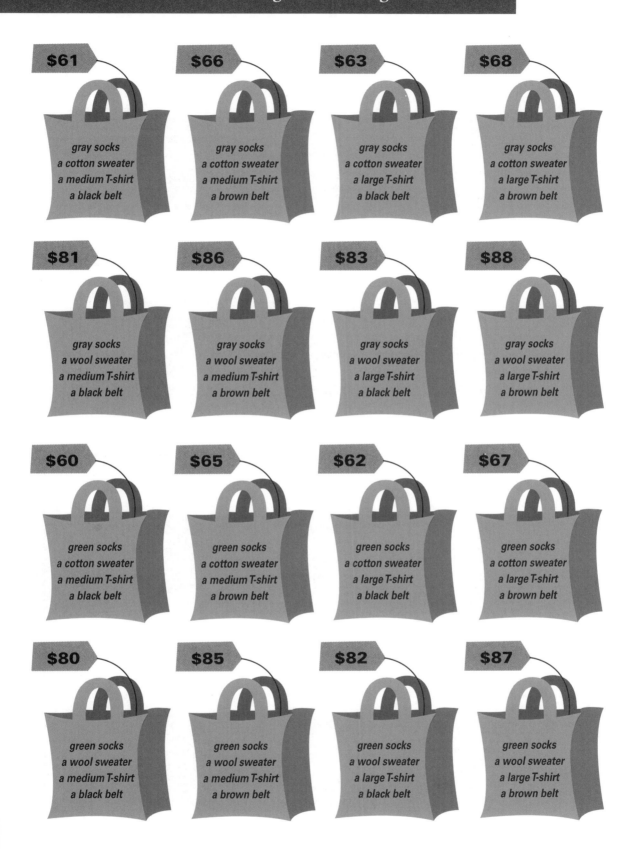

$61
gray socks
a cotton sweater
a medium T-shirt
a black belt

$66
gray socks
a cotton sweater
a medium T-shirt
a brown belt

$63
gray socks
a cotton sweater
a large T-shirt
a black belt

$68
gray socks
a cotton sweater
a large T-shirt
a brown belt

$81
gray socks
a wool sweater
a medium T-shirt
a black belt

$86
gray socks
a wool sweater
a medium T-shirt
a brown belt

$83
gray socks
a wool sweater
a large T-shirt
a black belt

$88
gray socks
a wool sweater
a large T-shirt
a brown belt

$60
green socks
a cotton sweater
a medium T-shirt
a black belt

$65
green socks
a cotton sweater
a medium T-shirt
a brown belt

$62
green socks
a cotton sweater
a large T-shirt
a black belt

$67
green socks
a cotton sweater
a large T-shirt
a brown belt

$80
green socks
a wool sweater
a medium T-shirt
a black belt

$85
green socks
a wool sweater
a medium T-shirt
a brown belt

$82
green socks
a wool sweater
a large T-shirt
a black belt

$87
green socks
a wool sweater
a large T-shirt
a brown belt

Exercise 20.   Speaking Activity: Who did what? There are two groups of names and actions. Student A should do one group, and student B should do the other group. In each group, there are seven names or pairs of names and seven actions.

Step 1.   Work in your area only (A or B). Draw lines to connect the seven subjects and seven actions. Mix up the lines. You will make seven new sentences. On the line (_____), write the past tense form. Follow the examples. For example, if student A draws a line from "Sammy" to "eat fish for dinner," then the new sentence in the past tense is "Sammy ate fish for dinner." Remember we are practicing past tense of irregular verbs.

Step 2.   Now work with a partner. You will ask questions about your partner's sentences in order to guess his or her seven sentences. Student A will ask about B's lines, and student B will ask about A's lines. For example, student A can ask, "Did Susan go to Miami?" If student B has a line from "Susan" to "go to Miami," then B says, "Yes, Susan went to Miami. That's correct." And it is still student A's turn to ask another question.

If student B does not have a line from "Susan" to "go to Miami," then B says, "No, Susan didn't go to Miami. That's not correct." And it is student B's turn to ask a question.

The winner is the first student to guess all seven of his or her partner's lines (sentences).

Student A

Sammy   go to the park ___went___

Maria   wake up at 6 A.M. _____

Paul   eat fish for dinner _____

Joe and Sue   lose a ten-dollar bill in the street _____

Mr. Mills   tell some jokes _____

Chang   send a letter to Paris last week _____

Julie   buy some fried chicken _____

Student B

Jonathan   make a chocolate cake ___made___

Susan   get up at 7 A.M. _____

Kirk   go to Miami _____

Tim and Bob   spend one hundred dollars on shoes _____

Mrs. Wilson   understand the math lesson _____

Pierre   sleep more than 8 hours last night _____

Mohamad   have a car accident _____

Exercise 21.   Multiple Choice. Circle the letter of the correct answer.

1. "Did Beth choose a gift for her mother's birthday?"

   "Yes, _____."

   (A) she did   (C) she was

   (B) they did   (D) they were

2. "What did you do yesterday?"

   "Not much. I _____ very busy."

   (A) didn't   (C) don't

   (B) wasn't   (D) weren't

3. "Did she _____ for today's test?"

   "No, she watched TV and talked on the phone instead."

   (A) studied   (C) study

   (B) studying   (D) studies

4. I gave the money to Jerry _____.

   (A) tomorrow   (C) usually

   (B) next week   (D) two days ago

5. The rain was very heavy, so I _____ the window.

   (A) was close   (C) close

   (B) was closed   (D) closed

6. We saw a movie last night. I liked it, but my friend Greg _____ it.

   (A) likes   (C) doesn't like

   (B) liked   (D) didn't like

7. "What's wrong? What's the problem?"

   "The test _____ really difficult. My score was only 53 out of 100."

   (A) did   (C) was

   (B) didn't   (D) wasn't

8. Joe: "Tom, the dinner tonight was excellent. Thanks so much!"

   Sue: "Yes, Tom, it was great. You always _____ so well."

   Tom: "Thank you both for the nice words. Please come again."

   (A) cook   (C) were you cook

   (B) cooked   (D) did you cook

Exercise 22.   Review Test

Part 1.   Write any correct verb in the blanks. Use the correct verb tenses. You will use some words more than one time.

watch	like	wash	taste	write	answer
clean	cook	explain	be	go	study

1. Every Friday night I _____ to my friend's house. His name

    _____ Rick. Some of our other friends usually come over, too. We

    usually _____ TV together. Last night we _____ a movie

    about monsters from another planet. Rick _____ it very much, but I

    _____ it. It _____ really bad.   ,

2. Emily and Susan _____ dinner last night for ten people. It

    _____ a special dinner. The food _____ great. After

    dinner, Bob and I _____ the dishes. George and Emma

    _____ the kitchen area.

3. Mr. Keyes is a very good teacher. I really _____ his class. He

    _____ difficult things to us. He _____ new words on the

    board for us. He _____ all our questions. Yesterday's class was really hard,

    but Mr. Keyes _____ the lesson very well. In that class, we

    _____ *ed* for past tense in English.

Part 2.   Read each sentence carefully. Look at the underlined part. If the under-lined part is correct, circle the word *correct*. If it is wrong, circle the wrong part and write the correct form above.

correct	wrong	1.	<u>Did you like</u> the movie last night?
correct	wrong	2.	The baby was very sick, so <u>she cryed</u> all night.
correct	wrong	3.	I <u>didn't want</u> to study last night, but it was necessary.
correct	wrong	4.	When <u>did your English class begin</u>?
correct	wrong	5.	<u>Do you work</u> for this same company last year?
correct	wrong	6.	I <u>make</u> scrambled eggs for breakfast yesterday.
correct	wrong	7.	The food was very bad. We <u>wasn't</u> like it very much.
correct	wrong	8.	<u>Did you and Harriet read</u> today's newspaper?

Unit 7

Wh- Questions

1. who
2. whom
3. what
4. when
5. where
6. why
7. which

Who is this?

What is in the box?

When was the test?

Where did you go?

Wh- Questions

What is that?
What is your name?
What do you eat for breakfast?
What did he study in college?

What
is for things.

When is the party? When do you study? When was the accident? When does your class begin?	**When** is for time.
Where were you yesterday? Where are the books? Where is your homework? Where do you live?	**Where** is for places.
Why are you tired? Why do you shop at that store? Why is she at the library now? Why did you do that?	**Why** is for reasons.
Who is the president of your country? Who are your best friends? Who played tennis with Mike? Who has my pencil?	**Who** is for people.
There are two books. Which do you want? There is a red car, a blue car, and a white car. Which car do you like? Which boy is your cousin?	**Which** is for people or things. (We use **which** when we have a choice.)

CAREFUL! Watch out for these common mistakes.

1. Do not forget to use correct grammar for questions (word order).
   wrong: What you have in that bag?
   correct: What do you have in that bag?

   wrong: When the final exam for grammar class is?
   correct: When is the final exam for grammar class?

2. Do not use the wrong question word.
   wrong: *Question:* When are India and Pakistan?
                    Answer: They are in Asia.
   correct: *Question:* Where are India and Pakistan?
                    Answer: They are in Asia.

   wrong: Which is your name?
   correct: What is your name?

Exercise 1. Fill in each blank with the correct question word: *who, what, when, where, which,* or *why.* Follow the example.

example: Q: ___Where___ is the green book?
A: It's <u>on the table</u>.

1. Q: __When__ is your test?

   A: It's <u>on Tuesday</u>.

2. Q: __Who__ washed the dishes?

   A: <u>Brenda</u> did.

3. Q: __Why__ did you go to the store?

   A: <u>Because I wanted some bread</u>.

4. Q: __What__ did you eat for lunch?

   A: <u>Beans and rice</u>.

5. Q: __When__ do you study?

   A: I study <u>at night</u>.

6. Q: __What__ is your favorite color?

   A: It's <u>dark green</u>.

7. Q: __What__ did you study last night?

   A: I studied <u>math and English</u>.

8. Q: __Where__ do you live?

   A: My house is <u>next to the park</u>.

9. Q: __Which__ shirt is your shirt?

   A: It's <u>the blue shirt on the chair</u>.

10. Q: __Who__ are your best friends?

    A: <u>Rachel and Gwen</u> are.

Exercise 2. Write a *yes-no* question and give a short answer. Then write a *wh-* question using *what* and give a short answer. (*Hint:* Change the underlined words to *what*.) Follow the example.

example: He writes <u>letters</u> every day.
(yes-no) ___Does he write letters every day?___
___Yes, he does.___
(what) ___What does he write every day?___
___Letters.___

1. Paul reads <u>mystery stories</u> on the weekend.

   (y-n) ___Does Paul reads mystery storie on the weekend ?___
   ___Yes, he does___

   (wh) ___What does he reads on the weekend ?___
   ___mystery stories.___

2. Tina is <u>a dentist</u>.

   (y-n) ___Is tina a dentist?___
   ___Yes, she is___

   (wh) ___what does Tina is. ?___
   ___a dentist___

3.   Victor studied <u>French</u> with Mark.

(y-n)   Did, Victor study french with Mark
         Yes, vheor did

(wh)   What did study with Mark ?
       French

4.   You like <u>tennis and football</u>.

(y-n)   Do you like tenis and Football ?
        Yes, I like.

(wh)   what do you like ?
      Tenis and football

Exercise 3.   Write a *yes-no* question and give a short answer. Then write a *wh-* question using *when* and give a short answer. (*Hint:* Change the underlined words to *when*.) Follow the example.

example: Karen wrote three letters <u>last night</u>.
       (yes-no)   <u>Did Karen write three letters last night?</u>
                <u>Yes, she did.</u>
       (when)   <u>When did Karen write three letters?</u>
                <u>Last night.</u>

1.   Victor began the work at <u>10 A.M.</u>

(y-n)   Did Victor begun the work at 10.am. ?
        Yes, Victor begon at 10 am

(wh)   When

2.   The girls watch a movie <u>every Friday night</u>.

(y-n)   Did girls watch a movie every Friday night
        Yes, they did.

(wh)   When did watch a movie ?

3. The big tennis tournament was <u>last weekend.</u>

   (y-n) _____

   _____

   (wh) _____

   _____

4. Laura takes a long walk <u>every Sunday morning</u>.

   (y-n) Does laura take a long walk every Sunday morning?

   (wh) When does laura takes a long walk every Sunday morning

---

Exercise 4. Write a *yes-no* question and give a short answer. Then write a *wh-* question using *where* and give a short answer. (*Hint:* Change the underlined words to *where*.) Follow the example.

   example: Mrs. Mills works <u>at the bank</u>.
   (yes-no) Does Mrs. Mills work at the bank?
   Yes, she does.
   (where) Where does Mrs. Mills work?
   She works at the bank.

1. You live <u>on Green Street</u>.

   (y-n) Do You live on Green Sreet
   Yes, I do.
   (wh) Where do you live?

2. They watched a movie <u>at Carl's house</u>.

   (y-n) Do they watch a movie at Carl's house?
   Yes, they'o
   (wh) Where did they watch a movie?
   they watched a movie at Carl's hous.

3. Zina and Ellen work <u>at the bakery</u>.

    (y-n) _Do Zina and Ellen work at the bakery?_
           Yes, they do

    (wh) _Where do Zina and Ellen work ?_

4. The books were <u>in the desk drawer</u>.

    (y-n) _Do were the books in the desk drawer?_
           Yes, they do

    (wh) _Where were the book?_
           in the desk Drawer.

Exercise 5.   Write a *yes-no* question and give a short answer. Then write a *wh-*question using *why* and give a short answer. (*Hint:* Change the underlined words to *why.*) Follow the example.

    example: She is tired now <u>because she worked all day</u>.
             (yes-no)   Is she tired because she worked all day?
                          Yes, she is.
             (why)   Why is she tired now?
                          Because she worked all day.

1. Victor speaks French <u>because he lived in France</u>.

    (y-n) _Does Victor speak french?_
           Yes Victor speaks French.

    (wh) _Why Victor speak French?_
           Becaus he lived in France.

2. Mark stayed home <u>because it was too cold to go outside</u>.

    (y-n) _Did Mark stay_

    (wh) _Why did Mark stay home?_
           because it was too cold to go outside.

3. You like volleyball <u>because it has a lot of quick points</u>.

   (y-n) _Do you like volleyball ?_

   _Ye_

   (wh) _Why do yo like volley ball?_

   because is has a fot of quick points.

4. Tina is a teacher <u>because she likes children</u>.

   (y-n) _Is Tina a teacher?_

   Yes, She is

   (wh) _Why is Tina a teacher ?_

   because she likes children.

Exercise 6.   Write a *wh-* question using *which* and give a short answer. (*Hint:* The underlined words are the answer to the question.) Follow the example.

   example: The book <u>on the table</u> is the teacher's book.
   Which book is the teacher's book?
   The book on the table.

1. The bread <u>on the top shelf</u> is on sale.

   Which bread is on sale ?

   on the top shelf

2. Question <u>number seven</u> was the most difficult.

   Which question was the most difficult ?

   number seven

3. You like <u>grammar</u> class the best.

   Wich class you like.?

   gramanar

4. <u>Those white</u> flowers come from Mexico.

   which flower come from Mexico ?

   those white flowers .

5. Of all the restaurants, he likes <u>McDonald's</u> the best.

   Wich of all the restaurant, he likes ?

Exercise 7.   Write a *wh-* question using *who* and give a short answer. (*Hint:* The underlined words are the answer to the question.) Follow the example.

> *example:*   <u>Mary</u> knows John.
> <u>   Who knows John?   </u>
> <u>   Mary does.   </u>

1. <u>Mr. Miller</u> is their grammar teacher.

   _____

   _____

2. <u>Joe</u> helped Alan with the homework.

   _____

   _____

3. <u>Pam and Bob</u> waited for Tom.

   _____

   _____

4. <u>Mrs. Yates</u> is a dentist.

   _____

   _____

5. <u>Wendy</u> talked to Pat.

   _____

   _____

FOR MORE ADVANCED STUDENTS

A Special Note about *Who*

Who can be singular or plural.
We can use **who** for one person, and we can use **who** for two or more people.

(a) Who <u>is</u> your <u>friend</u>?   = one friend
                                                 Friend does not have **s,** so we know
                                                 this is one person.

(b) Who <u>are</u> your <u>friends</u>?   = two or more friends
                                                 Friends has an **s,** so we know
                                                 there are two or more people.

In these two examples, a word (**friend** or **friends**) helps us to know the number of people.
• Use singular when a word in the sentence tells you that there is only one person.
• Use plural when a word in the sentence tells you that there are two or more people.
• This situation (= using a word to tell you singular or plural) is only true with **be** (and a few other verbs).

Who <u>is</u> at the door?   = one person or two people or ???
                                          We do not know the number of people.

Who <u>has</u> my watch?   = one person or two people or ???
                                          We do not know the number of people.

Who <u>lives</u> in that house?   = one person or two people or ???
                                          We do not know the number of people.

Who <u>is</u> on the telephone?   = one person or two people or ???
                                          We do not know the number of people.

In these examples, **no** word helps us to know the number of people.
• When no word in the sentence tells you the number of people, use a **singular** verb.
• We always use a singular verb with **who** (except with **be** and a few others): ha<u>s</u>, speak<u>s</u>, goe<u>s</u>.

FOR MORE ADVANCED STUDENTS

Exercise 8.   In each question, underline the correct verb form (singular or plural). For questions 6 through 10, if there is a word that tells you if *who* is singular or plural, circle that word. Follow the example.

example: Who (<u>is</u>, are) in your class?
               [We do not know the number of people.]
               Who (<u>is</u>, are) your favorite football (player?)
               [We know the number: 1.]
               Who (<u>knows</u>, know) the answer?
               [We do not know the number.]
               Who (is, <u>are</u>) those (boys?)
               [We know the number: plural.]

1.   Who (understand, understands) the teacher's explanation?

2.   Who (has, have) one dollar?

3.   Who (live, lives) in that house?

4.   Who (drive, drives) a white car?

5.   Who (was, were) at the party last night?

6. Who (is, are) your grammar teacher?

7. Who (is, are) your friends?

8. Who (is, are) your favorite singers?

9. Who (was, were) your teacher last year?

10. Who (is, are) he?

FOR MORE ADVANCED STUDENTS

Exercise 9.   In each question, underline the correct verb form (singular or plural). If there is a word that tells you singular or plural, circle that word. Follow the examples.

examples: Who (<u>is</u>, are) in your class?
Who (<u>knows</u>, know) the answer?

1. Who (understand, understands) this book?

2. Who (is, are) your favorite actors?

3. Who (drive, drives) a green car?

4. Who (was, were) at the meeting yesterday?

5. Who (is, are) your English teacher?

6. Who (is, are) your teachers?

7. Who (has, have) five dollars?

8. Who (live, lives) in that apartment?

9. Who (was, were) your favorite uncle?

10. Who (is, are) she?

11. Who (want, wants) some coffee now?

12. Who (is, are) on the telephone?

13. Who (is, are) your parents?

14. Who (is, are) your cousins?

15. Who (live, lives) in the White House?

16. Who (is, are) Bill and Hillary Clinton?

17. Who (go, goes) to school by bike?

18. Who (has, have) my books?

19. Who (play, plays) tennis every day?

20. Who (study, studies) the most?

OPTIONAL SECTION

Who/Whom

<u>Who</u> is at the door?   **Who** is the subject of the sentence.
<u>Who</u> passed the test?   (The subjects are underlined.)
<u>Who</u> called you last night?
<u>Who</u> has your umbrella?

Who was <u>president</u> in 1990?   **Who** is used when the verb is **be** and **who** and
(who = president)   the subject talk about the same person.★
Who are those <u>boys</u>? (who = boys)   (The subjects are underlined.)
Who is <u>she</u>? (who = she)

Whom do <u>you</u> play tennis with?   **Whom** is not the subject.
Whom did <u>Mark</u> visit?   (The subjects are underlined.)
Whom do <u>Rick and Sue</u> work with?
Whom did <u>you</u> call?
Whom does <u>Anne</u> study with?

★*Exception:* We use **whom** with **be** if there is a preposition: Whom are <u>you</u> for? (whom π you) Whom is <u>she</u>
with? (whom π she) Whom are they near? (whom π they)

Some teachers may wish to skip the section on *who* vs. *whom* (including Exercises 10–12) temporarily or
omit it completely according to the goals of the course (spoken English vs. written English) and the
language level of the students.

Exercise 10.   Underline the correct question words. Follow the examples.
     examples: (Who, <u>Whom</u>) did you go with?
                (<u>Who</u>, Whom) are your best friends?
                (<u>Who</u>, Whom) studied this lesson last night?

1. (Who, Whom) is your grammar teacher?

2. (Who, Whom) did Mark play tennis with?

3. (Who, Whom) speaks English the best?

4. (Who, Whom) do you see?

5. (Who, Whom) was at the party?

6. (Who, Whom) did the homework?

7. (Who, Whom) do you study with?

8. (Who, Whom) has my keys?

9. (Who, Whom) swims the best?

10. (Who, Whom) called you last night?

11. (Who, Whom) does Ahmad like?

12. (Who, Whom) knows the answer?

Exercise 11.   Write *who* or *whom* on the lines. Follow the example.

          example: __Who__   has my book?

1. _____ does Mary like?

2. _____ knows John?

3. _____ does he play tennis with?

4. _____ understands the lesson?

5. _____ did you ask?

6. _____ are your teachers?

7. _____ do you see?

8. _____ has my pen?

9. _____ needs a pencil?

10. _____ did the homework?

11. _____ knows the answer?

12. _____ was on your team?

Exercise 12.   Make questions using *who* and *whom*. Follow the example.

          example: Mr. Miller called Paul.
                     (who)   __Who called Paul?__
                     (whom)   __Mr. Miller called whom?__

1. Jane visited Martha yesterday.

     (who)   _____

     (whom)   _____

2. Ann studies with Matt.

     (who)   _____

     (whom)   _____

3. Ann and Bob study with Matt in the evening.

(who) _____

(whom) _____

4. John and Martha play tennis with Anne and Matt every day.

(who) _____

(whom) _____

5. The teacher waited for all the students.

(who) _____

(whom) _____

6. Ted knows Jack well.

(who) _____

(whom) _____

7. Carlos telephoned Keith.

(who) _____

(whom) _____

8. Jan has a class with Danny.

(who) _____

(whom) _____

What Does _____ Mean?

When you have a word that you do not know, ask someone.
The correct question to ask the meaning of a word is:

What does _____ mean?

Lee:	Excuse me, I want some doughnuts?	
Clerk:	How many do you want? Do you want a dozen?	
Lee:	*Dozen???* I don't know this word.	Lee does not know the meaning of *dozen.*
Clerk:	Do you want a dozen doughnuts?	
Lee:	What does *dozen* mean?	He asks the clerk the meaning.
Clerk:	It means "twelve." A lot of people buy a dozen doughnuts.	The clerk explains the word.
Lee:	OK, give me a dozen, please.	

Exercise 13.   Write a question for each word and then write the meaning. Use a dictionary or ask an English speaker. Follow the example.

example: dozen   *Question:*   <u>What does dozen mean?</u>
                       Answer: <u>Dozen means twelve.</u>

1. hard   Q: _____
             A: _____

2. sour   Q: _____
             A: _____

3. quantity Q: _____
             A: _____

4. a few   Q: _____
             A: _____

For 5 and 6, find a word that you do not know. Then find the meaning in a dictionary or from a native speaker.

5. _____   Q: _____
             A: _____

6. _____   Q: _____
             A: _____

Exercise 14.   Make a question by substituting *who,* why, what, when,* and *where* for the underlined words. Follow the examples.

examples: <u>Mary</u> called John. <u>Who called John?</u>
              He speaks <u>English</u> at home. <u>What does he speak at home?</u>

1. She arrives <u>at 8 A.M.</u>   _____

2. Mary learned French <u>in Paris</u>.   _____

3. She asked <u>John</u>.   _____

4. <u>Rick</u> wants a new car.   _____

5. Jane has <u>a new watch</u>.   _____

6. The boys are <u>in the kitchen</u>.   _____

*If you studied pages 107–9, use *whom* in some of the sentences.

7. The boys are in the kitchen.   _____

8. They go to Florida every summer.   _____

9. They go to Florida every summer.   _____

10. You played tennis with Mike.   _____

11. Yuri walks to school because

    she likes the exercise.   _____

12. Fiesta means a party.   _____

▬▬▬▬▬

Exercise 15.   Review of question words. Make questions according to the underlined words. Follow the example.

1. Mary studied French with Paul and Sue last night.
      A   B   C   D

   (A) _____ Who studied French with Paul and Sue last night? _____

   (B) _____

   (C) _____

   (D) _____

2. Hilarious means very funny.

   _____

3. Jill and Zina listen to the radio every night.
        A

   They do this because they want to learn new English words.
                            B

   (A) _____

   (B) _____

4. Thomas Edison invented the lightbulb. He was born in Ohio. He died in 1931.
            A   B   C   D

   (A) _____

   (B) _____

   (C) _____

   (D) _____

Exercise 16.   Scrambled Conversations. Put these conversations in the correct order by writing *1* next to the first line of the conversation, *2* next to the second line, and so on. Then take turns reading them with a partner.

Conversation 1

Person A

1   Hi, Susan. How are you?

___   The day after tomorrow.

___   Hey, maybe we can have lunch one day.

___   What about Thursday?

___   I have a big English test. I'm studying for it.

___   My class finishes at noon, so let's meet at 12:30.

___   Let's go to the Indian restaurant on Stern Street.

Person B

___   When is your test?

___   OK, when are you free for lunch?

___   Well, good luck on your test!

___   Good. See you there on Thursday at 12:30.

___   Sure, let's do that. Where?

___   OK. What time do you want to meet?

2   Fine, thanks. What are you doing with all those books?

Conversation 2

Person A

1   What's your name?

___   And where do you work now?

___   OK, let me read your resume again, and I'll call you.

___   When did you start working there?

___   And now you'd like to work for our company?

___   Why do you think that?

___   Larson's. What do you do there?

___   We will call everyone by Friday.

Person B

___   At Larson's Department Store.

___   OK, thank you for the interview. I hope to hear from you soon.

___   I'm a very hard worker, and I'm a quick learner.

___   When do you think you will call?

___   Andrew Lim.

___   I'm a sales clerk.

___   About five years ago, sir.

___   Yes, I think I can do a good job here.

Conversation 3

Person A   *Person B*

1 You look tired.   ___ Around 2:30.

___ What was your score on the test?   ___ I needed to study for my test today.

___ Which class do you have that in?   ___ Math.

___ Wow, that's pretty late. Why did   ___ I stayed awake until very late.
you do that?

___ What time did you go to sleep?   ___ Mrs. Sims. She always gives tough
                                                   tests.

___ Who is your math teacher?   ___ I don't know yet. I'll find out
                                                   tomorrow.

─────────

Exercise 17a. Speaking Activity—Student A. Five students from five different countries are studying English in the U.S. This chart has some information about these five students. However, some of this information is missing. Work with a partner to get the missing information.

Step 1. Work with a partner.

Step 2. One student is A and the other is B.

Step 3. A asks B about any square in the chart. Use *who, what, when,* and *where* in your questions. Pay close attention to question formation grammar. Reverse roles after each question.

Step 4. Good luck! (Do not look at the other page if you are A.)

Name	Student Number	Country	Born	Arrived in U.S.	Teacher
Susan Johnson	228441		Stockholm		Mr. Green
Katrina Gomez			Lima		
Brian Andros	219558		Athens	March 1995	
Paul Lee	223819	Taiwan			Mr. Mills
Emi Tanaka		Japan		last October	

Exercise 17b. Speaking Activity—Student B. Five students from five different countries are studying English in the U.S. This chart has some information about these five students. However, some of this information is missing. Work with a partner to get the missing information.

Step 1. Work with a partner.

Step 2. One student is A and the other is B.

Step 3. A asks B about any square in the chart. Use *who, what, when,* and *where* in your questions. Pay close attention to question formation grammar. Reverse roles after each question.

Step 4. Good luck! (Do not look at the other page if you are B.)

Name	Student Number	Country	Born	Arrived in U.S.	Teacher
Susan Johnson		Sweden		January 1995	
Katrina Gomez	228497	Peru		last year	Mr. Benson
Brian Andros		Greece			Ms. Jody
Paul Lee			Taipei	two years ago	
Emi Tanaka	228114		Tokyo		Ms. Valen

Exercise 18. Multiple Choice. Circle the letter of the correct answer.

1. "_____ French?"

   "In France."

   (A) When did study he

   (B) When did he study

   (C) Where did he study

   (D) Where did study he

2. "What _____?"

   "It means very big."

   (A) means huge

   (B) huge means

   (C) does mean huge

   (D) does huge mean

3. "_____ did you telephone?"

   "Last night."

   (A) When   (C) What means

   (B) Why   (D) Where

4. "_____ is your new address?"

   (A) Where   (C) What

   (B) Which   (D) Who

5. "_____ write letters to?"

   "John."

   (A) Whom you   (C) Who you

   (B) Whom do you   (D) Who do you

6. "When _____ ?"

   "At 10 A.M."

   (A) arrived he   (C) he arrived

   (B) did he arrive   (D) did arrive he

7. "_____ did you go there?"

   "Because we needed some milk."

   (A) When   (C) What

   (B) Where   (D) Why

8. _____ movie did you like the best?

   (A) Which   (C) What

   (B) Why   (D) When

Exercise 19.   Review Test

Part 1.   Fill in each blank with the correct word or words to complete these conversations.

1. *A:* _____ do you live?

    B: I live in Miami, Florida.

2. *A:* Who _____ your favorite actors?

    B: Stallone and Redford.

3. *A:* _____ were you late to class?

    B: Because I woke up late.

4. *A:* _____ did they watch?

    B: An old movie.

5. *A:* _____ is the test?

    B: It's next Friday.

6. *A:* What _____?

    B: It means light red.

7. *A:* Who _____ a book now?

    B: Mark, Susan, and I have a book.

8. *A:* When _____?

    B: I study at night.

Part 2.   Read each sentence carefully. Look at the underlined part. If the underlined part is correct, circle the word *correct*. If it is wrong, circle the wrong part and write the correct form above.

correct   wrong   1. *A:* <u>Where was</u> the meeting?

                              B: It was at 8 P.M.

correct   wrong   2. *A:* <u>What means this word</u>?

                              B: It means very cold.

correct   wrong   3. *A:* Who <u>wants</u> some coffee?

                              B: Susan and I want some coffee, please.

correct   wrong   4. *A:* <u>You study English in America why</u>?

                              B: Because I want to pass TOEFL.

correct   wrong   5. *A:* <u>Where does Marsha live</u>?

                              B: In an apartment near the university.

correct   wrong   6. *A:* <u>What do Victor has</u> in his bag?

                              B: A new radio.

Part 3.★ Underline the correct word.

1. (Who, Whom) did you see at the store?

2. (Who, Whom) are those boys by the window?

3. (Who, Whom) is your English teacher this year?

4. (Who, Whom) is in the room?

5. (Who, Whom) cooks every day?

6. (Who, Whom) has a pencil now?

★Teachers: Only classes that will be taught the *who/whom* distinction should do this section now.

Unit 8

Word Order

1. adverbs of place and time   2. adjectives before nouns

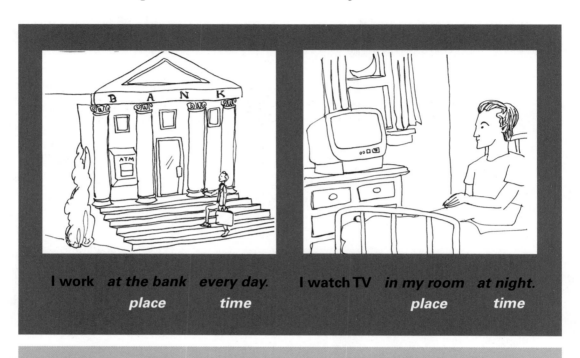

I work *at the bank* *every day.*
    place   *time*

I watch TV *in my room* *at night.*
    place   *time*

Adverbs of Place and Time

Place	*Time*
here	now
there	then
in the room	on Monday
at McDonald's	in July
near the bank	at 2:00 P.M.
on the table	next week

1. When there are two **adverbs of time** together or two **adverbs of place** together, we usually put the smaller one first. (Move from small to large.)

   The book is <u>on the table</u> <u>in the room</u>.

         small ⟶ big

   I have a test <u>at 10 A.M.</u> <u>on Monday</u>.

         small ⟶ big

2. When we have one adverb of place and one adverb of time, we usually put the adverb of place first. (Remember: P before T.)

I am studying <u>at this school</u> <u>this semester</u>.
                 1. place   2. time

The books were <u>on the table</u> <u>yesterday</u>.
               1. place   2. time

Note to advanced students: This is a very general rule to guide you in your English studies. You will find many exceptions to this rule.

CAREFUL! Watch out for these possible problems.

1. Remember to put small places before large places and small times before large times.
   strange: I live on Nebraska Street in a house.
   better: I live in a house on Nebraska Street.

   strange: The meeting will take place in the morning at nine.
   better: The meeting will take place at nine in the morning.

2. Be careful with the position of adverbs of place and time in a sentence. The usual order is place and then time. Sometimes you can change this, but in the beginning (you are a beginning student of English), it is better to remember: **place, then time.**
   strange: At the bank Mr. Miller works every day.
   better: Mr. Miller works at the bank every day.

   strange: I watched a movie last night there.
   better: I watched a movie there last night.

Exercise 1.   Write *place* or *time* on the lines to tell the type of adverb. Follow the examples.

examples: at 9:00 A.M.   <u> time </u>   in class <u> place </u>

1. in the library   _____
2. in the morning _____
3. at 7:00 A.M.   _____
4. in New York   _____
5. in ten minutes _____

6. at night   _____
7. here   _____
8. now   _____
9. at the store _____
10. every night _____

Exercise 2.   Write new sentences from the parts. Pay attention to the word order.   Follow the example.

example: every day/at home/The man has/dinner
          The man has dinner at home every day.

1. lunch/We eat/at noon/in a restaurant

   _____

   _____

2. at 10 A.M./They have/at the university/class

   _____

   _____

3. there/before class/I have/coffee

   _____

4. in the library/He studies/every night/French and math

   _____

5. She practices/every day/in the laboratory/pronunciation

   _____

6. to class/every day/They go

   _____

7. You drink/in the morning/milk/at the table

   _____

8. at night/in the library/letters/You write

   _____

9. every day/in class/She studies

   _____

10. to class/He comes/every afternoon

   _____

11. lunch/on Green Street/We eat/at a small table/in the Chinese restaurant

   _____

12. She practices/from 2 to 3/in the laboratory/pronunciation/on Mondays

   _____

13. in first class/Mr. Miller/on a 747/in an aisle seat/prefers to sit

_____

14. of four Canadians/within one hundred miles/Three/live/of the U.S. border

_____

Exercise 3. Speaking Activity: Building Correct Sentences

Step 1. Fill in the blanks to make some simple sentences. You need a subject and a verb. You need one place and one time, but you can have two places and/or two times. The number is up to you.

Step 2. Read the parts of one of your sentences to a partner. Mix up the parts. Do not read them in the order they are on your paper.

Step 3. Your partner has to tell you the correct sentence. If it is the same as the sentence on your paper, say "That's correct." If it is not, say, "Try again."

Step 4. After student B says student A's sentence correctly, then it is B's turn to read his or her sentence parts to A.

Note: It might be easier for student B to write down the sentence parts.

Subject	Verb	Object	Place 1	Place 2	Time 1	Time 2
Joe	eats	lunch			at noon	every day.
She	works		at the bank	on Gray Rd.	from 9 to 5.	

Homework: Write your sentences on a separate sheet of paper.

Adjectives

examples:	hungry	tired	tall	short
	cheap	expensive	smart	deep
	green	red	late	heavy

After be
I am <u>tired</u>.
She is <u>intelligent</u>.
The rings are <u>small</u> but <u>expensive</u>.
Everyone is <u>hungry</u> now.

Before nouns
That is a <u>beautiful</u> car.
A <u>black</u> cat climbed up the <u>big</u> tree.
The <u>grammar</u> test was a <u>difficult</u> exam.
Do you sell <u>green</u> sweaters here?

CAREFUL! Watch out for these possible problems.

1. Adjectives go in front of nouns.
    wrong: I live in a house small.
    correct: I live in a small house.

2. We do not have a plural form for adjectives in English. There is only one form.
    wrong: The books are expensives.
    correct: The books are expensive.

Exercise 4.   Underline the correct words. Follow the example.

> *example:*   This is a (<u>nice towel</u>, towel nice).

1. *A:* What is (your class first, your first class, class first your) every day?

    B: It's grammar.

    A: Do you like that class?

    B: Well, I have five classes every day. Four of them are (easy, easys), but grammar is a

    very (class difficult, difficult class) for me. It's hard, but I like it a lot.

2. *A:* Do you know Dr. Wong?

    B: Yes, she is (favorite professor my, my professor favorite, my favorite professor).

    A: Really?

    B: Yes, definitely. She's very kind, and she is extremely (intelligent, intelligents).

3. *A:* I have two (big sandwiches cheese, bigs cheese sandwiches, big cheese sand-

    wiches).

    Do you want one?

B: Yes, please give me one. What kind of cheese is it? Is it (cheese American, American cheese) or is it (Swiss cheese, cheese Swiss)?

A: Neither. It's just (cheese yellow, yellow cheese).

4. A: Who are the (people most important, most important people) in this company?

B: Well, I guess Miss Woods and Mr. Conrad are.

_____

Exercise 5.   Multiple Choice. Circle the letter of the correct answer.

1. We like to write letters. We write _____.

   (A) every day letters in our room   (C) in our room every day letters

   (B) letters every day in our room   (D) letters in our room every day

2. We have our _____ at 10 A.M.

   (A) here grammar class   (C) grammar class here

   (B) here class grammar   (D) class grammar here

3. The teacher _____.

   (A) on the board wrote his name   (C) wrote his name on the board

   (B) wrote on the board his name   (D) his name wrote on the board

4. Mr. and Mrs. Smith were married _____ in Toronto.

   (A) before one year   (C) there last year

   (B) ago one year   (D) last year there

5. "What is your present for Christina for her birthday?"

   "A pair of _____."

   (A) small gold earrings   (C) gold earrings smalls

   (B) earrings small gold   (D) smalls earrings gold

6. He goes _____ every day.

   (A) at 8 to the bank   (C) in the morning early

   (B) to the library at noon   (D) on Martin Street to the store

7. Which sentence is correct?

   (A) She is very now hungry.   (C) The chair green is not very old.

   (B) The books are very interestings.   (D) This new pencil has a pink eraser.

8. They like to eat _____.

   (A) at the restaurant Japanese on Madison Street

   (B) at the Japanese restaurant on Madison Street

   (C) on Madison Street at the Japanese restaurant

   (D) on Street Madison at the Japanese restaurant

Exercise 6.   Review Test

Part 1.   Read this short passage. There are five phrases that are unusual English. In these five phrases, the word order is a little strange. Circle the phrases and write the corrections above them.

This is Karla Reiss. She is working in her garden. On Pine Street she lives. She has a small house white. This house is very old. Karla was in 1959 born in this house. Both her parents died several years ago, and Karla is divorced. Now she lives alone. Karla keeps busy by doing many things different. She likes to work behind her house every morning in the small garden. She is very good at gardening. The flowers in her garden are very beautiful. Karla's neighbors tell her this all the time. Karla only smiles and says, "I didn't do anything. The flowers do all the work."

Part 2.   Put these sentence parts in the correct order. Write the new sentence on the line.

1. in a/house/lived/last/year/we/on Green Street/small

   _____

2. arrive/at school/most students/before nine

   _____

3. at 8 P.M./the next meeting/on March 7th/will take place*/in room 105

   _____

take place means to happen or occur: Another shooting took place on that bridge last night.

4. traveled/from Ontario/our teacher/

    and his family/to Nova Scotia

    _____

    _____

    _____

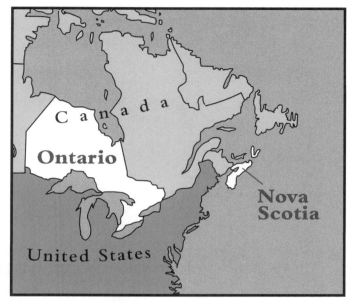

Part 3.   Read each sentence carefully. Look at the underlined
part. If the underlined part is
correct, circle the word
correct. If it is wrong, circle
the wrong part and write the
correct form above.

correct   wrong   1. The vocabulary books are <u>in the first room on the second floor</u>.

correct   wrong   2. Were you <u>on Wednesday night at 7 P.M. at John's party</u>? It was

                          great!

correct   wrong   3. Did you write your name <u>at the top of the page</u>?

correct   wrong   4. Please come <u>at noon here</u>.

correct   wrong   5. Does Marsha live <u>in an apartment near the university</u>?

correct   wrong   6. The magazines are <u>on the small table next to the sofa in the

                          living room</u>.

correct   wrong   7. Are the concert tickets <u>in Mike's desk in the top drawer</u>?

Unit 9

Present Progressive Tense

1. form: *be* + present participle
2. present participle spelling
3. affirmative
4. negative

5. questions
6. short answers
7. verbs that don't use present progressive
8. use in the future

Dear May,

Scott and I are in New York City. We are having a great time. We are spending a total of 7 days here.

I am visiting old friends. Scott and I are doing a lot of shopping, too. We are trying not to spend a lot of money.

We are staying at the Royal Sonesta. It's a nice hotel. I like it a lot.

Love, Ann

May Sawyer
833 Green St.
Fairfax, VA

Discover Grammar

1. Look at the sentences below. Some of them are correct, and some of them are wrong. Read the sentences and try to understand the grammar rule for these sentences.
2. Work with a partner. Discuss your ideas.

1. I go to work at Hills Bank every day. (correct)
2. I am going to school every day. (wrong)

3. My father is eating breakfast every day. (wrong)
4. My sister eats cereal for breakfast every day. (correct)

5. The students are reading their books right now. (correct)
6. The teachers teach English right now. (wrong)

7. I make tea when I'm thirsty. (correct)
8. I make tea now. (wrong)

9. I am making tea now. (correct)
10. I make tea now. (wrong)

11. In the summer it rains a lot. (correct)
12. Today it rains very hard. (wrong)

13. *Bob:* Are you busy?
    Joe: Yes, I study for my test. (wrong)
14. *Sue:* Are you busy?
    Tim: Yes, I'm cleaning the kitchen. (correct)

15. What are you doing now? (correct)
16. What do you do now? (wrong)

What is the grammar rule for this unit? _____

_____

_____

_____

Discuss your answer with a partner or in small groups. What are your ideas?

(The grammar rule for this unit is explained on pages 128–30.)

Present Progressive Tense of Verbs

Present

I **live** in an apartment.
You **walk** to class every day.
He usually **works** in the day.
She **studies** English here.
It **rains** a lot in the summer.
We sometimes **talk** about our problems.
They always **arrive** late.

Present Progressive

I **am living** in an apartment this year.
You **are walking** to class right now.
He **is working** now.
She **is studying** French in France this month.
It **is raining** hard, so we can't go out now.
We **are talking** about our problems now.
They **are arriving** right now.

simple present
This action is true all of the time.
This action happens many times.

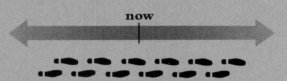

I usually walk to school.

present progressive
This action is happening now.

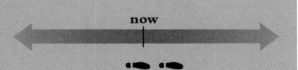

I am walking to school now.

simple past
This action is finished.
It happened one time or a few
times in the past.

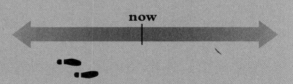

I walked to school yesterday.

Exception: We use present progressive only with verbs that show action.

action:	eat	drink	play	study	stand
	do	read	say	have a good time	
	listen	watch			
no action:	see	hear	own	possess	like	love
	need	want	seem	feel	be	prefer
	remember	forget	believe	have		

wrong: I am having two books now.
correct: I have two books now.

wrong: I am seeing TV now.
correct: I am watching TV now.

Now look at the examples on the next page.

	WORK	LIVE	STUDY	CUT
I	I am working	I am living	I am studying	I am cutting
you	you are working	you are living	you are studying	you are cutting
he	he is working	he is living	he is studying	he is cutting
she	she is working	she is living	she is studying	she is cutting
it	it is working	it is living	it is studying	it is cutting
we	we are working	we are living	we are studying	we are cutting
they	they are working	they are living	they are studying	they are cutting
		e—(+ ing)		**double consonant**

In the present progressive tense, there are two parts: **be** and the **ing** form (present participle).

For **be,** use **am, is,** or **are** according to the subject.

For the **ing** form, add **ing** to the base form of the verb.

Spelling rules:

1. Drop the final **-e** before adding **ing.** take → taking, write → writing
2. Double the final consonant if there is only one vowel before it.★ cut → cutting, begin → beginning
3. Do not double the final consonant if there is not one vowel before it. end → ending, keep → keeping, read → reading, close → closing

★Note to advanced students: If a word has two syllables and has only one vowel before the final consonant, we double the final consonant if the pronunciation stress is on the second syllable. be·gín → beginning
If a word has two syllables and has only one vowel before the final consonant, we do NOT double the final consonant if the stress is on the first syllable. ó·pen → opening

CAREFUL! Watch out for these common mistakes.

1. Don't use **VERB** or **VERB + s** for actions that are happening now.
    wrong: Laura cooks scrambled eggs for breakfast now.
    correct: Laura is cooking scrambled eggs for breakfast now.

    wrong: We study very hard for tomorrow's test.
    correct: We are studying very hard for tomorrow's test.

2. Don't use **ing** for actions that happen every day or all the time.
    wrong: I am studying English every day.
    correct: I study English every day.

    wrong: The earth is going around the sun one time in one year.
    correct: The earth goes around the sun one time in one year.

3. Don't forget to use **be.**
    wrong: My baby sister crying now.
    correct: My baby sister is crying now.

wrong: I reading this book right now.
correct: I am reading this book right now.

4. Be careful with the spelling of the participle forms.
    wrong: cuting, siting, planing, eatting, helpping, openning
    correct: cutting, sitting, planning, eating, helping, opening

5. Don't use present progressive if the verb does not show action.
    wrong: I am owning two cars.
    correct: I own two cars.

    Examples of verbs that are rarely in progressive form are: **own, possess,
    like, love, need, want, seem, feel, be, prefer, remember, forget, believe.**

    When **have** means "possess," it is not in progressive form. Use the simple form.
    wrong: I am having a car now.
    correct: I have a car now.

    When **have** means "do some kind of action," progressive form is OK.
    wrong: I have a party now.
    correct: I am having a party now.

Exercise 1.   Write the forms of *work* in present and present progressive tenses.
Follow the examples.

> *Present*   *Present Progressive*
>
> 1. I __work__ every day.   8. I _am working_ now.
>
> 2. You _____ at night.   9. You _____ right now.
>
> 3. He _____ all of the time.   10. He _____ today.
>
> 4. She _____ every day.   11. She _____ this week.
>
> 5. It _____ most of the time.   12. It _____ now.
>
> 6. We _____ every afternoon.   13. We _____ hard this semester.
>
> 7. They _____ here every day.   14. They _____ here now.

15. Now make a list of time expressions for these two verb tenses.
    First, copy the time expressions from sentences 1–14 onto the chart on page 131.
    Can you add any other time expressions to the lists?

Simple Present	*Present Progressive*
I work	I am working
you work	you are working
he works	he is working

Time Words

1. _____
2. _____
3. _____
4. _____
5. _____
6. _____
7. _____

Others:

Time Words

8. _____
9. _____
10. _____
11. _____
12. _____
13. _____
14. _____

Others:

Exercise 2.   Fill in the blanks with the correct forms of the verbs. Follow the examples.

Present Progressive

COUNT	TAKE	DRINK	RUN
I _am counting_	I _____	I _____	I _____
you _are counting_	you _____	you _____	you _____
he _____	he _____	he _____	he _____
she _____	she _____	she _____	she _____
it _____	it _____	it _____	it _____
we _____	we _____	we _____	we _____
they _____	they _____	they _____	they _____
Jo _____	Jo _____	Jo _____	Jo _____
Jo and I _____	Jo and I _____	Jo and I _____	Jo and I _____

10 sentence.

"My Summer vacation"

Exercise 3. Write each expression in the present progressive tense. Put an X by the verbs that you cannot use in present progressive.

1. you read _____
2. they like _____
3. you repeat _____
4. we ask _____
5. we go _____
6. it needs _____
7. I count _____
8. they type _____
9. I watch _____
10. you shout _____

11. she listens _____
12. I wait _____
13. he learns _____
14. they explain _____
15. she uses _____
16. you hear _____
17. she has _____
18. I shop _____
19. we prefer _____
20. he takes _____

Exercise 4. Write the correct form of the verb in each sentence. Follow the example.

example: (write) (A) The boys _are writing_ letters now.
(B) They _write_ letters once a week.

(read) 1. After I eat breakfast, I usually _____ the newspaper.

2. This week I _____ a book by Stephen King. It's scary.

(study) 3. Susan is busy now. She _____ math.

4. Susan _____ math for an hour every day.

(play) 5. Mark and I _____ tennis after school.

6. I can't play today, so Mark _____ with someone else.

(like) 7. Jenny didn't like coffee when she was a child, but now she really

_____ it a lot.

8. Jenny _____ to drink orange juice for breakfast.

(have) 9. We _____ a new house now.

10. We _____ a good time with the

swimming pool this summer.

(cook) 11. I can't play tennis with you now.

I _____ dinner.

12. I sometimes _____ rice with vegetables.

Exercise 5.   Sammy wrote a letter to his friend David. Read the letter and
underline the twenty-three subject and verb combinations. Write S
over the subjects and V over the verbs. The first one is already done
for you. Work with a partner. Try to explain why each verb is
present, past, or present progressive.

Dear Sammy,

         V   S   V
Hi, how <u>are you doing</u>? How are things there? I hope everything is going o.k.

I'm writing you this letter now because I want to give you my address. I have
some good news. I have a new place. Do you remember my old apartment? It
really wasn't so nice, but the rent was quite high. I finally decided to move. My
new address is 1706 East Powers Avenue. The city is the same of course.

Are you still working a lot? How is your boss, Mr. Chan? Can you say hello to
him for me? I talked to him for about an hour the last time I visited you at your
office. He's really a nice guy.

O.k., I'm going to bed now. It's really late, and I have to get up early tomorrow!

Sincerely,

David

More examples

be + VERB + ing

Affirmative Statements
I**'m eating** rice.
You **are playing** tennis with Bob.
He**'s reading** a book right now.
It **is raining** now.
We**'re going** to the store now.
They **are having** a great time in Paris.

Negative Statements
I **am not eating** potatoes.
You **aren't playing** tennis with Jim.
He **is not reading** a magazine right now.
It **isn't snowing** now.
We **are not going** to the bank now.
They**'re not having** a bad time in Paris.

For negative, you add the word **not.**
It's the same as the verb **be** (unit 1).

Yes-No Questions and Short Answers

A: **Are you and Jim eating** fried fish?   *A:* Wow! **Are you going** to the bank now?
B: Yes, we **are**. It's delicious.   *B:* Yes, I **am**. Do you want to go with me?

A: **Are we taking** this bus?   *A:* **Is it snowing** now?
B: No, we **aren't**. Our bus is different.   *B:* No, it **isn't**. It's not so cold.

For questions, you move **be** to the beginning of the question.
For short answers, you answer with subject and **be** (Yes, I am/No, I am not).
It's the same as the verb **be** (unit 1).

Exercise 6.   Write a question from the words given. Then write a short answer.
Follow the example.

example: Tina – play tennis – with Bob – now (NO)
              Is Tina playing tennis with Bob now?
              No, she isn't.

1.   Mark and Joe – study English – together (YES)

     _____

     _____

2.   I – sit – in your chair (YES)

     _____

     _____

3.   it – snow – now (YES)

     _____

     _____

4.   Victor – watch – football – on TV (NO)

     _____

     _____

5.   the teacher – talk about – the homework (YES)

     _____

     _____

Exercise 7.   Make a question from each statement. Decide if the verb in the statement is simple present tense or present progressive tense. This will help you write the question. Follow the example.

example: A. It's raining now.   <u>Is it raining now?</u>
              B. It rains a lot in summer.   <u>Does it rain a lot in summer?</u>

1. A. Jill swims five laps every day.   _____

    B. Jill is swimming in the pool now.   _____

2. A. Mr. Yoshida teaches history.   _____

    B. Mr. Yoshida is teaching Sue now.   _____

3. A. They're having a good time there.   _____

    B. They have a good time in that class. _____

4. A. It's snowing heavily now.   _____

    B. It snows a lot in January.   _____

5. A. Joshua takes a shower at night.   _____

    B. Joshua is taking a shower now.   _____

6. A. Mr. Po is preparing lunch.   _____

    B. Mr. Po prepares lunch every day.   _____

7. A. Henry and Mark are studying.   _____

    B. Henry and Mark study together.   _____

8. A. You are playing a match now.   _____

    B. You play tennis very well.   _____

Exercise 8.   Now write short answers for the questions in Exercise 7. Check them with a partner. Take turns reading your miniconversations. Follow the example.

example: A. Yes, <u> it is </u>.
              B. No, <u> it doesn't </u>.

1. A. Yes, _____.

    B. No, _____.

2. A. No, _____.

    B. No, _____.

3. A. Yes, _____.

    B. Yes, _____.

4. A. No, _____.

    B. Yes, _____.

5. A. Yes, _____.

    B. No, _____.

6. A. Yes, _____.

    B. Yes, _____.

7. A. No, _____.

    B. Yes, _____.

8. A. No, _____.

    B. Yes, _____.

Exercise 9.   Make a *wh-* question according to the answer that is given. Use these verbs: *hurry, call, play, write, cook, go.*

example: Q: What _are you writing_____?
             A: A letter to my grandmother.

1. Q: What _____?

    A: Scrambled eggs.

2. Q: Where _____?

    A: At the high school tennis courts.

3. Q: Why _____?

    A: Because I'm late for work.

4. Q: Who _____?

    A: I'm calling Susan. I want to ask her about the homework.

5. Q: Where _____?

    A: To the bank. I have to get some cash.

Exercise 10. Fill in the blanks with the correct forms of these verbs. If there is no form, put an X in the box. Follow the examples.

	Present		Present Progressive	
	Affirmative	Negative	Affirmative	Negative
1. I/work	I work	I don't work	I am working	I am not working
2. he/like	he likes	he doesn't like	✕	✕
3. they/want				
4. Bill/listen				
5. we/watch				
6. you/practice				
7. he/be				
8. I/play				
9. it/begin				
10. they/sing				
11. we/know				
12. he/explain				
13. I/answer				
14. she/prefer				
15. we/understand				

Exercise 11.   Speaking Activity: Questions about a Picture. Look at the picture below. Write ten questions about the people and things in the picture. Try to use present progressive tense. Write five questions that have a *yes* answer. Write five questions that have a *no* answer. Write the short answers. Then work with a partner. Take turns asking each other questions.

Yes Answers:

example: <u>Is the man eating a sandwich?</u>

1.

2.

3.

4.

5.

No Answers:

example: <u>Is the cat running?</u>

1.

2.

3.

4.

5.

Exercise 12.   Multiple Choice. Circle the letter of the correct answer.

1. Is the bus driver driving too fast?

    (A) No, he is driving.   (C) No, he is a driver.

    (B) No, he isn't.   (D) No, he is.

2. "_____ Jim and Sam study together every day?"

    "No, because they live in different parts of the city."

    (A) Are   (C) Is

    (B) Do   (D) Does

3. We like television. We are _____ a good movie right now.

    (A) seeing   (C) watching

    (B) listening   (D) going

4. Math class is very difficult for me. I _____ that class very well.

    (A) am not understanding   (C) do not understand

    (B) am not understand   (D) don't understanding

5. Oh, there's Jim. I _____ him now.

    (A) see   (C) am not see

    (B) am seeing   (D) don't seeing

6. "Where _____, Matt? I need you to help me."

    "Don't worry. I'll be back in just a minute."

    (A) do you go   (C) do you going

    (B) are you go   (D) are you going

7. Uncle Ned is _____ some hot tea now.

    (A) liking   (C) seeing

    (B) preferring   (D) drinking

8. "Where is Kevin?"

    "He's at Greg's house. They _____ football."

    (A) are playing   (C) playing

    (B) is playing   (D) play

Exercise 13.   Review Test

Part 1.   Fill in each blank with one of these words. Use each word one time. You might have to make some changes in the form of the word.

shine	sleep	play	smile	drink	eat
like	fly	blow	have	sit	be

There are six people in this picture. They are in the park. It

(1)_____ a beautiful day. The sun (2)_____. It

is a very windy day.

There is an old man. He (3)_____ a long beard. He

(4)_____ on the bench. I think he (5)_____.

There are two children near the big tree. They (6)_____ with a ball.

They (7)_____. They are very happy.

There is a small girl with her mother. The girl (8)_____ an ice

cream cone. The mother (9)_____ a soft drink. She doesn't have an

ice cream cone. Maybe this is because she (10)_____ ice cream.

There is a teenager near the other trees. He (11)_____ a kite. I think

the wind (12)_____ very hard.

Part 2.   Look at the underlined part in the sentence. If the underlined part is
correct, circle the word *correct*. If it's wrong, circle the wrong part and
write the correct form above.

correct   wrong   1. Mark likes TV. He<u>'s seeing</u> a TV show right now.

correct   wrong   2. <u>Does Linda going</u> to the bank now?

correct   wrong   3. Mr. Wendall <u>is teaching</u> French in room 301 right now.

correct   wrong   4. The boys <u>no are doing</u> their homework now.

correct   wrong   5. People in Canada <u>drive</u> on the right-hand side of the road.

FOR MORE ADVANCED STUDENTS

Present Progressive for Future Time

We use present progressive for actions that are happening now, but it is also OK to use
present progressive for future actions. In this case, it is important to say the time of the
action. This is very common in conversation.
A: Do you want to play tennis tomorrow?
B: Sorry, I can't. I'm studying with James tomorrow.

A: What time is Colin arriving?
B: He's arriving at 8.

A: What are you doing next Saturday?
B: I'm helping Susan with her paper for English class.

Unit 10

Count vs. Noncount

1. *a/an* vs. *some/any*   3. *many* vs. *much* vs. *a lot*
2. *some* vs. *any*   4. *a few* vs. *a little*

a / some

a cat

some cats

an / some

an apple

some apples

a few / many, a lot

a few books

many books
a lot of books

a little / much, a lot

a little money

$12

much money
a lot of money

$1,000,000

Count Nouns/Noncount* Nouns

There are two groups of nouns: **count** and **noncount**.

Count nouns are nouns that we can count. **Book** is a count noun because we can say 1 book, 2 books, 10 books. Count nouns have a singular and a plural form.

Noncount nouns are nouns that we cannot count. **Water** is a noncount noun because we can not say 3 waters or 8 waters. Noncount nouns have only one form.

Count		Noncount
Singular	*Plural*	
a boy	some boys †	some water †
a question	10 questions	some cake
1 car	2 cars	some ink
1 book	some books	some paper
an orange	2 oranges	some fish
an umbrella	2 umbrellas	some furniture
1 child	4 children	some money
1 man	2 men	some bread
1 time	5 times	some time

Note:

The plural of most nouns is with **s**.

cat — cats   book — books

However, some nouns have irregular plural forms and do not use **s**.

man — men	woman — women
child — children	foot — feet
tooth — teeth	police officer — police
shelf — shelves	loaf — loaves
mouse — mice	

Note:

If you want to talk about one of a **noncount noun,** sometimes we can use a special word to help us:

a loaf of bread	a piece of cake
a sheet of paper	a bottle of oil
a slice of pie	a cup of coffee
a glass of milk	a bag of sugar

*Some books call these **mass nouns.**
†The word **some** means we do not know the number or the number or amount is not important. It is common to use **some** in front of a noncount noun. For example, people say, "Please give me some water." It is not usual to say, "Please give me water."

CAREFUL! Watch out for these common mistakes.

1. Do not put **a** or **an** with noncount nouns.
    wrong: The teacher gave us a homework for tomorrow.
    correct: The teacher gave us homework for tomorrow.

    wrong: Don't forget to buy a butter at the store.
    correct: Don't forget to buy some butter at the store.

2. Do not use the singular count form without **a, an, my, the,** etc. You must use something before it.

wrong:	Telephone has receiver and cord.
correct:	A telephone has a receiver and a cord.

wrong:	My cat has very long tail.
correct:	My cat has a very long tail.

wrong:	Teacher is going to give big test tomorrow.
correct:	The teacher is going to give a big test tomorrow.

Exercise 1. Count? Noncount? Write *C* by the count nouns and *NC* by the noncount nouns. Follow the examples.

___C___ book   ___NC___ water   ___NC___ ice

1. _____ banana
2. _____ chair
3. _____ air
4. _____ apple
5. _____ ink

6. _____ soup
7. _____ stamp
8. _____ butter
9. _____ milk
10. _____ radio

11. _____ pencil
12. _____ money
13. _____ dollar
14. _____ salt
15. _____ student

Exercise 2. *a? an? some?* Read the list of words. If the word is a count noun, write *a* or *an* on the line. If the word is a noncount noun, write *some* on the line. Follow the examples.

___an___ apple   ___some___ rice

1. _____ bed
2. _____ floor
3. _____ child
4. _____ problem
5. _____ money
6. _____ cookie
7. _____ coin
8. _____ furniture
9. _____ luggage
10. _____ ice

11. _____ number
12. _____ homework
13. _____ bill
14. _____ information
15. _____ banana
16. _____ car
17. _____ list
18. _____ line
19. _____ juice
20. _____ machine

Exercise 3. Read the list of words. If the word is a count noun, write a number on the line and add an *s.* If the word is a noncount noun, write *some* on the line.

1. _____ salt   11. _____ mail

2. _____ shirt   12. _____ trouble

3. _____ snow   13. _____ jar

4. _____ flight   14. _____ meat

5. _____ engine   15. _____ parent

6. _____ oil   16. _____ soup

7. _____ truck   17. _____ shoe

8. _____ soap   18. _____ fact

9. _____ egg   19. _____ suit

10. _____ problem   20. _____ trip

Exercise 4. *a? an? some?* Write *a, an,* or *some* on the line. Follow the example.

> *example:* *A:* Excuse me. I'm looking for __*a*__ book about Mexican cooking.
> *B:* OK. There are __*some*__ books about food over there on that table.
> *A:* Thanks.

1. *A:* I cooked _____ soup today.

   B: What kind is it?

   A: Vegetable. I put _____ macaroni in it.

   B: That sounds good. Give me just _____ small bowl, please.

2. *A:* I have _____ problem.

   B: What is it?

   A: I have _____ Malaysian money that I want to change to U.S. dollars.

   B: So what's the problem?

   A: Where can I change Malaysian money?

   B: Hmmmm. I think there is _____ international bank downtown near the river.

   There are _____ banks near the park, but they are small and I don't think they can

   change Malaysian money there. Try the international bank first.

A: I don't know it.

B: Yes, you know it. It's on State Street. There's _____ travel agency on the left and

_____ office on the right.

A: Oh, I know the place.

B: Do you have _____ Malaysian money with you now? What color is it?

A: I only have _____ coins with me now. You can look at them if you want.

3. *A:* We have _____ very difficult assignment for English for tomorrow.

B: We have _____ hard homework for our English class, too. What's your homework?

A: We have to read _____ stories and then answer ten questions about the material.

B: Well, we don't have to read so much, but we have

_____ exam tomorrow.

4. *A:* The next time I go to the store, I want to buy _____

apples.

B: What do you mean? There are _____ apples in the

refrigerator now.

A: No, someone ate the last apple.

B: That's strange. When I opened the refrigerator door about an

hour ago, I'm sure that I saw _____ apples on the top shelf of the refrigerator.

5. *A:* Dr. Sims, I really need _____ help with my paper. Do you have _____ time now

to help me?

B: I'm afraid I only have _____ minute.

A: Well, that's not enough, so maybe I can make _____ appointment to see you

later. I really need _____ help right away.

▬▬▬▬▬
Exercise 5.   Speaking Activity: Nouns from the Alphabet

Step 1.   Make a list of count nouns. The nouns should begin with the letters below.
           If you cannot think of a word, skip it and go on to the next letter.

A _____   E _____   I _____

B _____   F _____   J _____

C _____   G _____   K _____

D _____   H _____   L _____

M _____ R _____ V _____

N _____ S _____ W _____

O _____ T _____ Y _____

P _____ U _____ Z _____

Step 2.   Are the above items in this room? If the noun is actually in this room, circle the letter. If there is one of the items in the room, then write *a* in front of the noun. If there are more than one, write the number in front of the noun and then add the letter *s* to the noun.

Step 3.   Now work with a partner. Student A will name one of the letters from the exercise above. Student B will say the noun* he or she wrote for that letter. Then student A has to make a true sentence about the quantity of that item in the room.

A: "P"
B: pen
A: There are about 17 pens in this room. Now it's your turn.
B: "D"
A: duck
B: There isn't a duck in this room. Now it's your turn.
    (There are no ducks in this room. OR *There aren't any ducks in this room.)*
A: "T"
B: teacher
A: There is only one teacher in this room.

*If you aren't sure if a noun is count or noncount, put a check mark by it and ask your teacher later.

There is/There are

1. Use **there is** when the subject is singular or a noncount noun.
   Use **there are** when the subject is plural.

   There is a book here.
   There is some meat here.
   There are some books here.
   There are ten people here.

2. Usually the subject comes after the verb.

   There is a car in the driveway.

Some and *Any*

We use **some** and **any** with plural count nouns and with noncount nouns.
We use **some** and **any** when the number is not known or is not important.
Joe: "Would you like some tea?"
Tim: "Yes, give me some tea, please. I'm really thirsty."

Joe: "Do you have any coins? I need a quarter for the telephone."
Tim: "Sorry, I don't have any."

Joe: "Do you have some gum?"
Tim: "No, I don't have any gum right now. Sorry."

affirmative statement	*some*	I need some help.
negative statement	*any*	I don't need any help.
question	*some* or *any*	Do you need some help?
		Do you need any help?

Exercise 6.   Underline the correct words. Sometimes two answers are possible.

example: *A:* I want to buy a soft drink.
               B: There's a drink machine over there.
               A: Yes, but I don't have (some, <u>any</u>) change. Do you?
               B: No, but ask that woman over there. Maybe she has
                    (<u>some</u>, any).

1. *A:* Where's Sue?

    B: She went to the store.

    A: For what?

    B: She wanted (some, any) chocolate.

    A: But we have (some, any) in the refrigerator.

    B: No, we don't . . . Sorry, I ate all of it last night!

2. *A:* I cooked fried chicken for dinner. Do you want (some, any)?

    B: No, thanks.

    A: It's really pretty good. Are you sure?

    B: I'm a vegetarian.

    A: Really? I didn't know that.

    B: Yes, it's true. Sorry, but I can't eat (some, any) of the chicken.

3. *A:* Would you like (some, any) tea?

    B: Yes, that sounds good.

    A: Do you want (some, any) cream in it?

    B: No, thanks.

4. A: Did Kevin buy (some, any) apples yesterday?

    B: I don't think so. There aren't (some, any) here.

    A: Are you going to the store later?

    B: Maybe. Why?

    A: If you go, please get (some, any) apples for me.

    B: Sure. No problem.

5. A: Who cooked this soup?

    B: I did. Why?

    A: Well, there isn't (some, any) salt in it.

    B: Salt's bad for you, so I never put (some, any) in.

    A: Well, I need to have a little in this soup.

Exercise 7.   Write *some, any,* or *some/any* on the line. Follow the example.

> *example:*   A: Where are you going?
>   B: To the bookstore. I want to buy __*some*__ books.

1. A: I'm thirsty.

    B: Well, there's _____ iced tea in the refrigerator.

    A: No, I don't want to drink _____ drinks with caffeine.

    B: Well, I can make _____ lemonade if you want.

    A: Hey, that sounds great. Thanks.

2. A: Excuse me. I'd like to buy _____ Swiss cheese.

    B: Oh, I'm sorry, but we don't sell _____ cheese.

    A: OK, thanks.

3. A: Hi, come on in!

    B: Hi, I hope you're not busy right now.

    A: No, it's fine. Sit down. Would you like _____ coffee? It's fresh.

    B: I would love _____ coffee right now, but I can't drink

    _____.

    A: I don't get it. What do you mean?

    B: My doctor told me to stop drinking coffee.

A: Why?

B: I'm getting too much caffeine. I can't sleep at night.

4.   *A:* So what kind of food are you making for the party

   tomorrow night?

B: I'm making _____ sandwiches.

A: That's all? What about cookies or cake?

B: No, I'm not going to make _____ desserts. Sandwiches are easy to

   make.

A: Do you have everything already?

B: Yes, I went to the store this morning. I bought _____ bread,

   _____ lettuce and tomatoes, and of course _____ cheese

   and _____ meat.

A: Wow, it sounds like you are well prepared for the party.

B: Are you coming?

A: Sure. I'll be there.

B: Do you have _____ ideas for party games? If you do, let me know.

A: OK, I'll think about it, but I'm not very good at party games.

Many, Much, a Lot

We use **many** with *plural count nouns.*
We use **much** with *noncount nouns.*
We use **a lot** of with *count* and *noncount nouns.*

Sue: "Do you have any coins? I need seven quarters."
Zina: "Sorry, I don't have many, so I can't give you seven."

Joe: "Is Susan's family rich?"
Tim: "Yes, they are. They have a lot of money."

Bill: "We're going to be late for class."
Ann: "Yes, we need to hurry. We don't have much time."

	Count	Noncount
affirmative statement	a lot of —	a lot of —
	many —	—
negative statement	a lot of —	a lot of —
	many —	much —
question	a lot of —	a lot of —
	many —	much —

Remember: Do not use **much** + **NOUN** in affirmative statements.
wrong: I have much money.
correct: I have a lot of money.

Exercise 8.   Write *many* or *much* on the line. Follow the example.

        example: My wife and I don't drink __much__ coffee

1. That store has _____ interesting books.

2. Mrs. Sims is rich. She has _____ money.

3. We don't have _____ time now, so let's hurry.

4. I don't have _____ money now, so I can't go on the trip.

5. Wow, this office doesn't have _____ furniture in it.

6. _____ people attended the party.

7. Greg has three jobs, so that's why he always has _____ cash.

8. She's a very nice person and has _____ friends.

9. Did you read _____ books when you were in high school?

10. Do people in your country eat _____ red meat?

11. In _____ countries, taxis are yellow.

12. Cooking soup doesn't take _____ time.

13. Cooking stew takes _____ time.

14. We have _____ rain in winter but only a little in summer.

15. Can you go to the movie? Do you have _____ homework?

Exercise 9.   Underline the correct forms. Sometimes two answers are possible.
Follow the examples.

> *examples:*   He has (<u>many</u>, <u>a lot of</u>) friends.
> He has (much, <u>a lot of</u>) money.

1. *A:* Do you have (many, a lot of) old books?

    B: Yes, I do. I collect old books for a hobby.

2. *A:* Do you like this class?

    B: Yes, but there are (many, a lot of) words that I don't understand.

3. *A:* He didn't buy (much, a lot of) sugar at the store.

    B: That's because he doesn't like sweet foods.

    A: He didn't buy (many, a lot of) vegetables at the store either.

    B: Well, that's because he is trying to gain weight. He's too thin.

4. *A:* Mary, your coffee is almost white!

    B: Yes, that's true. I really like (much, a lot of) milk in my coffee.

5. *A:* Where did Sammy and Ahmed go?

    B: They went to the store.

    A: Why?

    B: They are going to make fruit salad for the party, so they are going to buy (much, a
    lot of) fruit at the store.

6. *A:* I'm really worried about the final exam.

    B: Why? There's (much, a lot of) time between now and the final exam.

    A: I want to make 100!

Hint: Look at your answers above. How many times did you underline *a lot of?* You can
see that *a lot of* is always possible (affirmative, negative, and question). You can see that
many is always possible, too. The problem is *much*. If this is still difficult for you, it might
be a good idea for you to use *a lot of* all the time. It's always correct.

---

a Few, a Little

We use **a few** with *plural count nouns.*
We use **a little** with *noncount nouns.*

Sue: "Do you have any coins? I need seven quarters."
Zina: "Sorry, I have a few, but I can't give you seven."

Joe: "Would you like something to drink?"
Tim: "Yes, give me a little coffee, please."

	Count	Noncount
affirmative statement **negative statement** **question**	{ a few —	{ a little —

Exercise 10.   Write *a few* or *a little* on the lines. Follow the examples.

        examples: __a few__   books   __a little__   coffee

1. _____ tea   7. _____ countries   13. _____ people

2. _____ time   8. _____ homework   14. _____ questions

3. _____ tests   9. _____ pencils   15. _____ bread

4. _____ ink   10. _____ children   16. _____ times

5. _____ paper   11. _____ classes   17. _____ water

6. _____ cream   12. _____ money   18. _____ furniture

Exercise 11.   Underline the correct forms. Follow the examples.

        examples: He has (<u>a few,</u> a little) nice ties.
                  He has (a few, <u>a little</u>) money.

1.   *A:* Do you have (a few, a little) coins? I want to make a phone call.

     B: How much money do you need?

     A: Just (a few, a little). I'm only going to talk for three minutes, so I only need about

        75 cents.

2.   *A:* How did you do on yesterday's exam?

     B: I only understood (a few, a little) questions. I guess I failed.

     A: I had (a few, a little) trouble with the first part, but I think I did OK on the second

        part.

3.   *A:* What did you buy at the store?

     B: (A few, A little) sugar and (a few, a little) vegetables.

4.   *A:* How does Suzana take her coffee?

     B: She likes (a few, a little) milk in it.

5. *A:* What's Billy going to do this weekend?

   B: He might read (a few, a little) books.

   A: Read books on the weekend? Why?

   B: Well, his research paper is due next Thursday. That means he only has (a few, a little) days to finish reading the books and then write the paper.

6. *A:* Do you have any plans for tomorrow?

   B: No, not yet. Why do you ask?

   A: Well, I'm going to the beach with (a few, a little) friends. Would you like to come with us?

   B: Gee, that sounds great. Thanks for inviting me.

   A: Be sure to bring (a few, a little) food with you, or you can bring (a few, a little) money and buy something there. We'll be there all day long.

Exercise 12.   Underline the correct quantity words. Follow the example.

   example: He wants (many, <u>a little</u>) sugar for his coffee.

1. I don't have (much, many) books. Let's go to the library.

2. You need (a few, a little) money if you want to buy something to eat.

3. What's she making? Why does she need (a lot of, a few) sugar?

4. Don't buy any pencils. We have (a lot of, much) pencils at home. We can give you some.

5. She has (a few, much) pencils, so she doesn't have to buy any.

6. Bob never buys (much, a few) milk because he lives alone.

7. We don't need to go to the store now. There is (much, a lot of) meat in the refrigerator.

8. We always buy (a lot of, a few) coffee because we drink it all the time.

9. They prefer (many, a lot of) sugar in their coffee, but I don't.

10. People in some Asian countries eat (much, a lot of) rice.

11. The doctor asked me, "Do you usually eat (a few, much) red meat?" Then he told me, "Don't eat (many, much) red meat. It's not good for your body."

12. It's not good to eat (many, a lot of) oily food.

Exercise 13. Speaking Activity: Are You Going to Buy . . . ? Work with a partner. You are going to go grocery shopping. Your shopping list is on the left. You are going to try to guess your partner's shopping list.

Step 1. Your list is on the left. Underline one of each pair of words in parentheses. This will make your list unique.

Step 2. Student A will begin by asking about student B's list. Begin with number 1. Ask "Are you going to buy a lot of meat?" or ask "Are you going to buy a little meat?" Student B will answer, "Yes, I am going to buy . . . " or "No, I am not going to buy . . . . " (You can mark the answers about your partner's list on the list at the right below.)

Step 3. If the answer is *yes,* then student A continues with number 2. If the answer is *no,* then student B can ask a question about number 1.

Step 4. The winner is the first person to guess the other student's entire list.

Your List	*Your Partner's List*
1. (a lot of, a little) meat	1. (a lot of, a little) meat
2. a few (apples, bananas)	2. a few (apples, bananas)
3. (a few, a lot of) potatoes	3. (a few, a lot of) potatoes
4. much (bread, spaghetti)	4. much (bread, spaghetti)
5. (much, a little) rice	5. (much, a little) rice
6. (a little, a lot of) flour	6. (a little, a lot of) flour
7. (a few, many) oranges	7. (a few, many) oranges
8. (a lot of, a little) mustard	8. (a lot of, a little) mustard
9. some (pickles, onions)	9. some (pickles, onions)
10. any (cookies, doughnuts)	10. any (cookies, doughnuts)

Exercise 14. Multiple Choice. Circle the letter of the correct answer.

1. "Do you like coffee?"

   "Oh, yes. I drink _____ coffee every day."

   (A) a lot of   (C) many

   (B) much   (D) any

2. "Do you need a lot of sugar?"

   "No, I only need _____ sugar."

   (A) a few   (C) any

   (B) a little   (D) much

3. "Would you like some tea?"

   "Yes, but just _____, please."

   (A) some   (C) a few

   (B) much   (D) a little

4. "You look tired."

   "Yes, I ran here. I'd really like _____ water."

   (A) much   (C) a few

   (B) a lot   (D) some

5. "What did you buy?"

   "I bought a loaf of _____."

   (A) bread   (C) cheese

   (B) meat   (D) sugar

6. "Who drew this picture?"

   "My son did. He's only four years old. In the picture, you can see two _____."

   (A) rice   (C) tooth

   (B) mice   (D) foot

7. "Is there anything on the table?"

   "Yes, there is a _____."

   (A) notebooks   (C) magazine

   (B) dictionaries   (D) slices of pie

8. "I need a pencil for my test."

   "Oh, I think there is _____ pencil in my briefcase. Let me check."

   (A) some   (C) a

   (B) any   (D) an

Exercise 15.   Review Test

Part 1.   Fill in the blanks with one of these: *many, much, a few, a little, some, any, a lot of.*

1. *Bill:*   "Would you like _____ tea?"

   Mark: "Thanks. I'm not very thirsty, so just give me _____."

Bill: "Do you want _____ cream in your tea."

Mark: "No, I don't want _____ cream, thanks. But I would like _____ sugar."

2. *Ann:* "Do you think that Mr. Thomson is rich?"

   Sue: "Yes, he has _____ money. He owns _____ shops in the down-town area."

3. *Paul:* "Did you go to the beach yesterday?"

   Mike: "Yes, I did."

   Paul: "How was it?"

   Mike: "I didn't have a good time. There were _____ people there. I don't like it when the beach is so crowded."

4. *Jim:* "Where did you go?"

   Ben: "To the grocery store."

   Jim: "Hey, did you remember to buy _____ potato chips for me?"

   Ben: "Sorry, I didn't buy _____ potato chips. I forgot."

   Jim: "That's OK. I'll get _____ the next time I go to the store."

   Ben: "I think there are _____ chips in the cabinet."

   Jim: "No, I looked this morning. There aren't _____ chips in the cabinet."

Part 2. Read each sentence carefully. Look at the underlined part. If the under-lined part is correct, circle the word *correct*. If it is wrong, circle the wrong part and write the correct form above.

correct	wrong	1.	She has <u>many</u> good friends at that school.
correct	wrong	2.	Would you <u>like any cheese now</u>?
correct	wrong	3.	He worked very hard, and now he <u>has much money</u>.
correct	wrong	4.	The science teacher gave us <u>a few homeworks</u>.
correct	wrong	5.	Kevin gave <u>Jim many old</u> newspapers.
correct	wrong	6.	There's <u>a slice of</u> cherry pie in the refrigerator.
correct	wrong	7.	Linda <u>has beautiful new car</u>.
correct	wrong	8.	She didn't <u>buy some fruit</u> at the store.

Unit 11

Prepositions

1. place   2. time

Place

I work at Lincoln Bank   *on Maple Street*   *in San Francisco.*

at _____   on _____   in _____

Time

I was born at 7:36 A.M.   *on September 11*   *in 1968.*

at _____   on _____   in _____

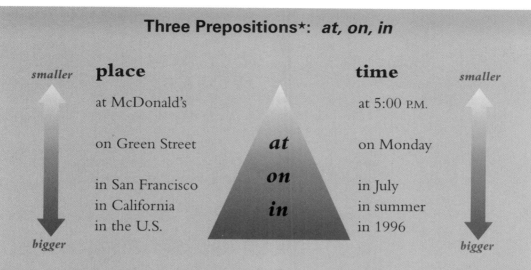

Three Prepositions*: *at, on, in*

place

smaller ↑

at McDonald's

on Green Street

in San Francisco
in California
in the U.S.

bigger ↓

time

at 5:00 P.M.

on Monday

in July
in summer
in 1996

smaller ↑

bigger ↓

at on in

Learn these phrases: in the morning
in the afternoon
in the evening
at night

1. Use **at** for very specific places or times.

Place Use **at** with the name of a place or with an address with a number.
   (A) He studies <u>at</u> Boston University.
   (B) I live <u>at</u> 653 Maple Drive.

Time Use **at** with clock times.
   (C) Please come <u>at</u> noon.
   (D) The class ends <u>at</u> 1:20.

2. Use **on** for "medium" size places or times.

Place Use **on** for streets, roads, avenues, etc., when there is no number.
   (E) I live <u>on</u> Maple Drive.
   (F) There were many cars <u>on</u> the highway yesterday.
   (G) Los Angeles <u>is</u> on the Pacific Coast.

Time Use **on** with days.
   (H) His birthday is <u>on</u> March 15th.
   (I) What did you do <u>on</u> Saturday?

3. Use **in** for large size places or times.

Place Use **in** for cities, states, and countries.
   (J) They live <u>in</u> Paris.
   (K) We grew up <u>in</u> Florida.
   (L) Florida is <u>in</u> the South.
   (M) Moscow is <u>in</u> Russia.

Place We also use **in** for all rooms.
   (N) Bill is not here now. He's <u>in</u> the kitchen.
   (O) You can sleep <u>in</u> the front bedroom.

*At, on,** and **in** are small words, but they are very common.

Time	Use **in** for months, seasons, and years.
	(P) The weather is hot <u>in</u> July.
	(Q) The weather is hot <u>in</u> the summer.
	(R) I was born <u>in</u> 1979.

Compare (B) and (E). In (B), there is a house number. (B) is more specific.

CAREFUL! Watch out for these common mistakes.

1. Do not forget to use a preposition.
   - wrong: My sister is England now.
   - correct: My sister is in England now.

2. Do not use **at** with years or with cities or other big places.
   - wrong: I was born at 1967.
   - correct: I was born in 1967.

   - wrong: San Francisco is at California.
   - correct: San Francisco is in California.

3. Don't forget about **on.** Many students don't use **on** correctly. Use **on** with street names when there is no house number and with days.
   - wrong: He lives at Maple Street.
   - correct: He lives on Maple Street.

   - wrong: I called Sam in his birthday.
   - correct: I called Sam on his birthday.

   - wrong: We played tennis at Friday night.
   - correct: We played tennis on Friday night.

4. Do not use **in** with days, streets, or specific names of places.
   - wrong: Katie doesn't work in Monday.
   - correct: Katie doesn't work on Monday.

   - wrong: The teacher's house is in Lincoln Road.
   - correct: The teacher's house is on Lincoln Road.

   - wrong: I work in Burger King.
   - correct: I work at Burger King.

5. Be careful with prepositions for parts of the day.
   - wrong: My class is at 8 at the morning.
   - correct: My class is at 8 in the morning.

   - wrong: I watch TV in the night.
   - correct: I watch TV at night.

Exercise 1.   Underline the correct prepositions.

1. (at, on) Monday   6. (in, at) the morning   11. (at, on) 12:30

2. (at, in) night   7. (at, in) 9   12. (at, on) Friday night

3. (at, on) Green Street   8. (at, in) 9 in the morning   13. (in, on) 1995

4. (at, on) 445 Green Street   9. (in, on) Saturday   14. (on, at) Green Street

5. (in, on) my birthday   10. (at, in) March   15. (at, on) March 17th

Exercise 2.   Underline the correct prepositions.

1. (at, on) Saturday   6. (in, at) the afternoon   11. (at, on) noon

2. (at, in) night   7. (at, in) 3   12. (at, on) Monday night

3. (at, on) Brown Road   8. (at, in) 3 in the afternoon 13. (in, on) 1996

4. (at, on) 200 Brown Road   9. (in, on) Tuesday   14. (on, at) my street

5. (in, on) the first day   10. (at, in) September   15. (at, on) January 1st

Exercise 3.   Write the correct prepositions. When you finish, copy your answers
on the correct lines. Then write the rules in the box.

1. _in_ Canada   6. _____ Paris   11. _____ 1993

2. _____ Main Street   7. _____ the summer   12. _____ 10 A.M.

3. _____ the kitchen   8. _____ May 11   13. _____ your birthday

4. _____ McDonald's   9. _____ Highway 883   14. _____ Texas

5. _____ Monday   10. _____ May   15. _____ December

at   *on*   *in*

at _____   on _____   in ___Canada_____

at _____   on _____   in _____

                                on _____   in _____

                                on _____   in _____

                                on _____   in _____

                                                               in _____

                                                               in _____

                                                               in _____

Use *at* with	Use *on* with	Use *in* with
		countries

Exercise 4. Write the correct prepositions. When you finish, copy your answers on the correct lines. Then write the rules in the box.

1. _____ Mexico

2. _____ September 11

3. _____ Burger King

4. _____ 2127 Hills Street

5. _____ Hardee's

6. _____ Bob's Used Cars

7. _____ noon

8. _____ Friday

9. _____ Dairy Queen

10. _____ Panama

11. _____ Thailand

12. _____ Cayuga Road

13. _____ 1988

14. _____ 7 P.M.

15. _____ 1776

at

at _____

at _____

at _____

at _____

at _____

at _____

at _____

on

on _____

on _____

on _____

in

in _____

in _____

in _____

in _____

in _____

Use *at* with	Use *on* with	Use *in* with

Exercise 5. Read these review notes. Then complete the sentences by writing in the correct missing prepositions.

Time Review: at/on/in

At is used with clock time (a specific time): at noon, at 4:30.
also: at night, at the beginning, at the end

On is used with days: on Monday, on July 7.
also: on Friday morning

In is used with general parts of the day: in the morning, in the afternoon.
In is used with months, seasons, and years: in May, in spring, in 1995.

1. She was born _____ December 9th _____ 1889.

2. In history class, we always have a test _____ Friday.

3. I still can't believe that he called me _____ 3:30 _____ the morning!

4. The trees this year were especially beautiful. _____ August they were full of green leaves, but _____ the fall they all turned to red or yellow.

5. English class starts _____ eight and ends _____ eight-fifty.

6. Many people take vacation _____ the summer, but I prefer to take mine _____ October.

7. The next meeting will be held _____ the third Saturday _____ February.

8. Though meetings are usually held _____ the morning, the next one will be _____ night.

9. The treaty between Russia and the U.S. will expire _____ midnight _____ the last day of this year.

10. When I saw Tina _____ lunch today, she looked very worried, but when I talked to her later _____ the afternoon, she said nothing was wrong.

Exercise 6.   Read these review notes. Then complete the sentences by writing in the correct missing prepositions.

Place Review: *at/on/in*

At is used with specific places, including street addresses:
at McDonald's, at 704 Green Street, at the corner of Green and Main.

On is used with street names: on Green Street, on Kennedy Avenue.
On is used when something touches a surface: on the wall, on the floor.

In is used with towns, cities, states, and countries: in Miami, in Canada.
In is used when something is inside: in the box, in my pocket.

---

1. The new post office is _____ Elm Road, but the old one was _____ the downtown
    area.

2. She was born _____ a suburb of Boston, but she grew up _____ Los Angeles.

3. He put his credit card _____ his wallet, and then he put his wallet _____ his back
    right pocket.

4. The saucers are _____ the top shelf of the white cabinet _____ the kitchen.

5. He used to live _____ 536 Goode Street, but now he lives _____ a different address.

6. I know you can get a money order _____ a bank, and I think you can get one
    _____ a convenience store, too.

7. Orlando is _____ Florida. Disney World is _____ Orlando.

8. Susan did a crossword puzzle on the bus today. She
    wrote the last word _____ the correct squares just as
    the bus arrived _____ the station.

9. She put the turkey _____ the oven and then
    checked the two pots _____ the stove.

10. I have worked _____ the appliance store _____
    Mills Avenue for six years.

11. (*Difficult:* good luck!) _____ that country, the people who
    live _____ the central part and the people who live _____ the coast speak with very
    different accents.

Exercise 7a. Speaking Activity: Student Information—Student A. Two students work together. Take turns asking each other questions about the information that is missing from the boxes below. Student A works on this page. Student B works on the next page.

Questions: When was (Paul) born?
Where was (Marjory) born?
What does (Paul) do?
Where is (the place)?
What times does he/she start work?
Who was born in 1963?

Name	Year Born	Where Born	Workplace	Location	Starting Time
	1970				7:00 A.M.
Paul		New York		Ben Road	
		Atlanta		Peach Street	3:00 P.M.
	1963		Star Taxi Co.★		11:00 P.M.
Marjory	1950		Nation's Bank		

★*Co.* is the abbreviation (short form) of *company.*

Exercise 7b.   Speaking Activity: Student Information—Student B. Two students work together. Take turns asking each other questions about the information that is not in the boxes below. Student B works on this page. Student A works on the previous page.

Questions: When was (Vick) born?
                 Where was (Tasha) born?
                 What does (Hank) do?
                 Where is (the place)?
                 What times does he/she start work?
                 Who was born in 1960?

Name	Year Born	Where Born	Workplace	Location	Starting Time
Vick		Miami	McDonald's	Main Street	
	1960		Nation's Bank		9:00 A.M.
Tasha	1975		Delta Airlines		
Hank		Dallas		Coral Street	
		Memphis		Branch Road	9:00 A.M.

Exercise 8.   Partner Drill

Step 1.   Choose ONE of the groups below.
Step 2.   Write the numbers 1 to 8 on the lines. Mix up the numbers (so everyone is not doing the same question at the same time).
Step 3.   Write the answers for *one* of the groups below.
Step 4.   Then work with a partner. Take turns drilling each other.
Step 5.   When you finish, work with a different partner.

example with Student A using Group 1 and Student B using Group 3:
                 A: "January"
                 B: "in January"
                 A: "That's right."
                 B: "night"
                 A: "in night"
                 B: "No, that's not right. Try again: night."
                 A: "at night"
                 B: "Yes, that's right."

Group 1	Group 2	Group 3
__. ___ 1997	__. ___ Monday	__. ___ night
__. ___ 2 P.M.	__. ___ the shelf	__. ___ May
__. ___ the evening	__. ___ fall	__. ___ winter
__. ___ January	__. ___ the afternoon	__. ___ 1945
__. ___ the kitchen	__. ___ 6 A.M.	__. ___ midnight
__. ___ First Union Bank	__. ___ the bathroom	__. ___ Tuesday
__. ___ Miller Road	__. ___ 1776	__. ___ the bedroom
__. ___ Saturday	__. ___ Young Avenue	__. ___ Ponte Street
__. ___ the last day	__. ___ Sam's Market	__. ___ Pizza Hut
__. ___ summer	__. ___ December	__. ___ Friday

Exercise 9. Multiple Choice. Circle the letter of the correct answer.

1. "When do you usually call Susan?"

"At 9 _____."

(A) in the night (C) at the night

(B) in night (D) at night

2. "Where is Joe now?"

"He's at the bank on _____."

(A) New York City (C) Green Street

(B) California (D) Nation's Bank

3. "Where do you work?"

"_____ Lucky Travel Agency."

(A) In (C) On

(B) At (D) To

4. "Let's play tennis at _____."

"OK, that sounds like a good idea to me."

(A) 5:30 (C) the morning

(B) Saturday (D) June 15

5. "Where are Mark and Katie?"

   "They're _____ the kitchen."

   (A) in   (C) on

   (B) at   (D) to

6. "What do students usually do _____ the first day of school each year?"

   "Sometimes they write essays about what they did in the summer."

   (A) in   (C) on

   (B) at   (D) to

7. "Where does Benjamin live?"

   "He lives on _____."

   (A) 536 Broad Street   (C) Miami

   (B) Broad Street   (D) Miami, Florida

8. Which one of these is correct?

   (A) at spring   (C) at Friday night

   (B) at noon   (D) at Kennedy Avenue

Exercise 10.   Review Test

Part 1.   **Read these sentences. Fill in the blanks with *at, in,* or *on.***

1. They have a new baby. She was born _____ First General Hospital _____ June 17th.

2. *Geography teacher:*   "Where are Moscow, Vancouver, and Manila?"

   Student: "Moscow is _____ Russia, Vancouver is _____ Canada, and Manila is _____ the Philippines."

3. There are two libraries _____ my town. One library is _____ 2447 George Street, and the other library is _____ the First Plaza Building _____ Wendy Road.

4. Does it snow a lot _____ your country _____ the winter?

5. What do you usually do _____ your birthday?

Part 2. Read each sentence carefully. Look at the underlined part. If the underlined part is correct, circle the word *correct*. If it is wrong, circle the wrong part and write the correct form above.

correct	wrong	1. Vancouver is a city <u>on</u> British Columbia.
correct	wrong	2. Do you think that the best burgers are <u>in</u> McDonald's?
correct	wrong	3. It's impossible for her to arrive here <u>in</u> the afternoon.

correct	wrong	4. John is my best friend. I met him <u>in</u> 1992.
correct	wrong	5. I'm going to Texas <u>in</u> Friday.
correct	wrong	6. They have a TV <u>in</u> the living room and another <u>in</u> the kitchen.
correct	wrong	7. Fatima studied French <u>in</u> a small town near Paris.
correct	wrong	8. My first class is early <u>on</u> the morning.
correct	wrong	9. The bus will leave exactly <u>in</u> noon.
correct	wrong	10. The TV commercial said, "<u>In</u> Bob's Used Cars, we have the very best prices!"

Unit 12

Review

1. negatives
2. *yes-no* questions
3. short answers
4. *wh-* questions
5. demonstrative words
6. quantity words
7. verb tenses
8. prepositions

Exercise 1.   Negatives. Write the correct form. Use each word in the box one time.

| aren't | wasn't | don't | am not | didn't |
| doesn't | didn't | wasn't | wasn't | isn't |

1. September _____ have 31 days.

2. Columbus _____ travel around the world 10 times.

3. Mexico _____ a British colony.

4. California _____ one of the first states.

5. Alaska _____ a small state.

6. The first U.S. president _____ Abraham Lincoln.

7. I _____ British. Both my parents are American citizens.

8. In our school, 70 is a passing score. My score on the test yesterday was 65. I _____ pass the test.

9. People in Italy and Singapore _____ speak the same language.

10. Ghana, Egypt, and Nigeria _____ in Asia.

Exercise 2.   Speaking Practice (Negatives: *am not, isn't, aren't, don't, doesn't*). Write two things that are similar and one that is different. Tell which is different. Then write a reason why it is different. Follow the example.

example: __cat__   __green__   __bird__
Reason: __Green is different. It isn't an animal.__

When you finish your lists and reasons, work with a partner. Tell your partner your first list. Your partner must tell you what is different and the reason it is different. (You read your number 1 and your partner answers. Then your partner reads his number 1 and you answer. Take turns.)

1. _____   _____   _____

   Reason: _____

2. _____   _____   _____

   Reason: _____

3. _____   _____   _____

    Reason: _____

4. _____   _____   _____

    Reason: _____

5. _____   _____   _____

    Reason: _____

6. _____   _____   _____

    Reason: _____

7. _____   _____   _____

    Reason: _____

8. _____   _____   _____

    Reason: _____

Exercise 3.   Negatives. Can you complete this crossword puzzle with the correct eight words? There are twenty-seven clues to help you. Each clue has a blank. Fill in the blank with the correct **negative** word. Then use the clues to complete the puzzle. Work with a partner. Good luck! (*Hint:* Use *isn't* 12 times, *doesn't* 7, *don't* 5, *aren't* 3, and *didn't* 1.)

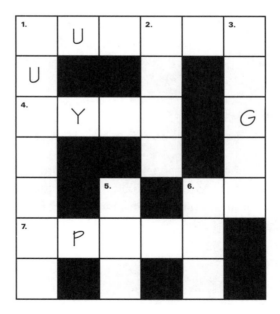

Across

1. A. This animal _____ big.

   B. It _____ move fast.

   C. People _____ eat this animal often.

4. A. They _____ purple.

   B. People _____ have 3 of these things.

   C. They _____ for hearing.

6. A. This word _____ long.

   B. This word _____ have many letters.

   C. This word _____ a noun or a verb.

7. A. The weather _____ cold in this month.

   B. This month _____ have six letters.

   C. I traveled to England in the summer.

   I_____ travel in this month.

Down

1. A. This _____ the name of a month.

   B. Classes _____ begin on this day.

   C. This day _____ come after Friday.

2. A. Students _____ like this thing.

   B. If it is hard, students _____ pass it.

   C. Sometimes it _____ easy.

3. A. This _____ a letter of the alphabet.

   B. This number _____ more than nine.

   C. This number _____ less than seven.

5. A. A man _____ use this title.

   B. This _____ a complete word.

   C. Jan _____ married. She _____

   put this title before her name.

6. A. This word _____ a verb or a noun.

   B. The 3 letters _____ 3 different letters.

   C. The word _____ have a good meaning.

Exercise 4.   Multiple Choice. Circle the letter of the correct answer. (Negatives: *am not, isn't, aren't, wasn't, weren't, don't, doesn't, didn't; yes-no questions*)

1. "Did you call your mom and dad yesterday?"

   "Yes, I did, but they _____ home when I called."

   (A) am not   (C) don't

   (B) weren't   (D) didn't

2. "Janice lives in an apartment."

"No, that _____ true. Janice lived in an apartment before, but now she lives in a house."

(A) isn't (C) don't

(B) aren't (D) doesn't

3. "How was your test?"

"Well, I _____ study, so my score was really bad."

(A) wasn't (C) isn't

(B) am not (D) didn't

4. "How was your vacation? Did you like Toronto?"

"We _____ there very long, but it was great!"

(A) doesn't (C) weren't

(B) am not (D) wasn't

5. "Was the test very long?"

"No, it wasn't. It _____ have so many questions."

(A) didn't (C) isn't

(B) wasn't (D) weren't

6. "That word is very long."

"No, this word _____ have many letters."

(A) am not (C) don't

(B) doesn't (D) isn't

7. "OK, let's go to the game room. I have one dollar."

"Only one dollar? One dollar _____ enough money."

(A) doesn't (C) isn't

(B) am not (D) don't

8. "_____ you study for the grammar test last night?"

"Yes, of course. Grammar class is difficult, so I studied for about 3 hours."

(A) Were (C) Do

(B) Was (D) Did

9. "Were you and Sally at the party last night?"

"No, we _____. Sally was sick, and I was tired."

(A) didn't   (C) weren't

(B) wasn't   (D) don't

10. "Excuse me. _____ you know what time it is now?"

"Yes, it is exactly 11 A.M."

(A) Is   (C) Do

(B) Did   (D) Are

11. "_____ you and your parents travel to France last year?"

"Yes, we did. It was a great trip."

(A) Did   (C) Are

(B) Was   (D) Were

12. "_____ the word dozen mean the same as twelve?"

"Yes, dozen and twelve mean the same thing."

(A) Is   (C) Does

(B) Are   (D) Do

13. "Do people in Brazil speak Spanish?"

"No, _____. Portuguese is the national language."

(A) it isn't   (C) it doesn't

(B) they don't   (D) they aren't

14. "_____ your score on the test the best in your class?"

"No, Jane had 10 more points than I did."

(A) Is   (C) Was

(B) Were   (D) Did

15. "_____ British Columbia and Ontario part of Canada in 1800?"

"No, I don't think so."

(A) Were   (C) Was

(B) Do   (D) Did

Exercise 5. Speaking Activity: Which Bag Is Yours? *(Yes-no* Questions: am, is, *are, do, does.)* Look at the shopping bags on page 177. Work with a partner. Your partner will choose one of these sixteen bags. Your task is to guess your partner's bag. You do this by asking *yes-no* questions. *Remember:* Use questions that begin with *do/does* or with *be.* Follow the example.

Step 1. Choose a bag that is yours. Look at what is in your bag.

Step 2. Student A asks a question about what is in B's bag: "Do you have shoes in your bag?"

Step 3. Student B gives a **true** short answer.

Step 4. If the answer is YES, then student A continues with another question: "Are the socks green?" or "Do you have green socks in your bag?"

Step 5. If the answer is NO, then it is B's turn to ask A a question.

The first student to guess his or her partner's bag is the winner.

> *example:* A: Do you have a belt in your bag?
> B: Yes, I do.
> A: Is the belt black?
> B: No, it isn't.
>
> B's answer was no, so A's turn ends. Now B can ask a question.

Exercise 6. Yes-No Questions: *am, is, are, was, were, do, does, did.* Draw lines to make correct questions. Follow the example.

Group 1

1.	Was	Washington and Kennedy from New York?
2.	Did	I in your seat?
3.	Am	they hungry now?
4.	Do	he late to class yesterday?
5.	Are	Paris in southern France?
6.	Were	cars cost a lot in your country?
7.	Is	you visit him 2 weeks ago?
8.	Does	any country have 2 capital cities?

Which bag is yours?

A:
gray socks
a cotton sweater
a striped shirt
a black belt

B:
gray socks
a cotton sweater
a medium T-shirt
a brown belt

C:
gray socks
a cotton sweater
a large T-shirt
a black belt

D:
gray socks
a cotton sweater
a striped shirt
a brown belt

E:
brown shoes
a wool sweater
a medium T-shirt
a black belt

F:
black shoes
a wool sweater
a medium T-shirt
a brown belt

G:
brown shoes
a wool sweater
a large T-shirt
a black belt

H:
black shoes
a wool sweater
a large T-shirt
a brown belt

I:
green socks
a cotton sweater
a medium T-shirt
a black belt

J:
green socks
a cotton sweater
a medium T-shirt
a brown belt

K:
green socks
a cotton sweater
a large T-shirt
a black belt

L:
green socks
a cotton sweater
a large T-shirt
a brown belt

M:
black shoes
a wool sweater
a striped shirt
a black belt

N:
brown shoes
a wool sweater
a medium T-shirt
a brown belt

O:
black shoes
a wool sweater
a large T-shirt
a black belt

P:
brown shoes
a wool sweater
a striped shirt
a brown belt

Group 2

9.   Do   it very cold last night?

10.   Are   your name have 5 or 6 letters in it?

11.   Did   your children happy when they opened their gifts?

12.   Were   you tired? If you aren't tired, let's play tennis!

13.   Am   you understand French? Can you translate this?

14.   Does   this your sweater?

15.   Is   you study? I was really busy last night, so I didn't have

                            time to study.

16.   Was   I right? I think your name is Suzanne Smith.

Exercise 7.   Short Answers: *am, is, are, was, were, do, does, did.* Write the possible short answers. Follow the example.

1.   Are the new students from Germany?

     Yes, ____they are_____. OR No, ____they aren't_____.

2.   Did it rain a lot yesterday morning?

     Yes, _____. OR No, _____.

3.   Do students at your school wear a uniform?

     Yes, _____. OR No, _____.

4.   Was your birthday this year on a Monday?

     Yes, _____. OR No, _____.

5.   Does this month have 31 days in it?

     Yes, _____. OR No, _____.

6.   Am I in your seat?

     Yes, _____. OR No, _____.

7.   Did you understand the homework?

     Yes, _____. OR

     No, _____.

8.   Is Thomas the best soccer player in this school?

     Yes, _____. OR

     No, _____.

9. Are the books on sale today?

   Yes, _____. OR No, _____.

10. Were you and I in the same math class in junior high school?

   Yes, _____. OR No, _____.

Exercise 8.   *Wh-* Questions: *who,* what, where, when, why, which.* Make questions according to the underlined words.

1. The U.S. became independent <u>in 1776</u>.

   _____

2. Stream means <u>a small river</u>.

   _____

3. The teacher arrives early <u>because she wants to write some things on the board</u>.

   _____

4. <u>Thomas Edison</u> invented <u>the lightbulb</u>. He was born <u>in Ohio</u>. He died <u>in 1931</u>.
          A   B   C   D

   (A) _____

   (B) _____

   (C) _____

   (D) _____

5. <u>The teacher</u> wrote a letter to <u>the boy's parents</u>.
          A   B

   (A) _____

   (B) _____

*Use *whom* in some sentences if your teacher tells you to do this.

Exercise 9.   Demonstratives: *this, that, these, those.* Underline the correct word.

1. *(John is at Mark's house. John sees an old book and picks it up. Mark is sitting in a chair about eight feet away.)*

   John: Mark, what is (this, that, these, those)?

   Mark: (These, That, This, Those) is an old book. My grandfather gave it to me.

   John: What are (this, these) red numbers on the cover?

   Mark: (These, Those) numbers? "6-4-58"? (Those, These) numbers mean the date when he gave it to me, June 4th, 1958.

2. *(Ann is about ten feet away from Bill. Bill is holding some cards in his hands.)*

   Ann: What are (that, those)?

   Bill: (This, These) are baseball cards.

   Ann: What are they for?

   Bill: I collect them. It's my hobby.

   Ann: Wow, (these, that) card in your right hand looks really old.

   Bill: Yes, it is. It's more than forty years old.

3. *(Ken and Pat are shopping in a department store.)*

   Ken: Do you like these (sweater, sweaters)?

   Pat: I think they look OK.

   Ken: Well, what about this (sweater, sweaters)?

   Pat: I like that a lot, but how much is it?

Exercise 10.   Quantity Words: *some, any, a few, a little, much, many, a lot of.* Underline the correct word. Sometimes there is more than one answer possible.

1. *A:* Why are you going to the store now?

   B: I want to buy (some, any, much, many) coffee.

   A: We have (any, a lot, some, a few) coffee here.

   B: No, there isn't (many, some, any) coffee. The jar is empty.

2. *A:* Excuse me. Do you have (some, much, any, a lot) books about Mexican history?

   B: We don't have (some, a lot). We only have (a little, a few, any).

A: Please show (some, much, a lot of) to me.

B: OK. Here you are.

3.   *A:* Excuse me. Could you give me (many, some, a few) help?

    B: I'm sorry, but I don't have (a lot of, many, some, much) time right now.

    A: I don't need (any, much, some, a few) time. It will take only (some, a few, much)

      minutes.

    B: Oh, OK. How can I help you?

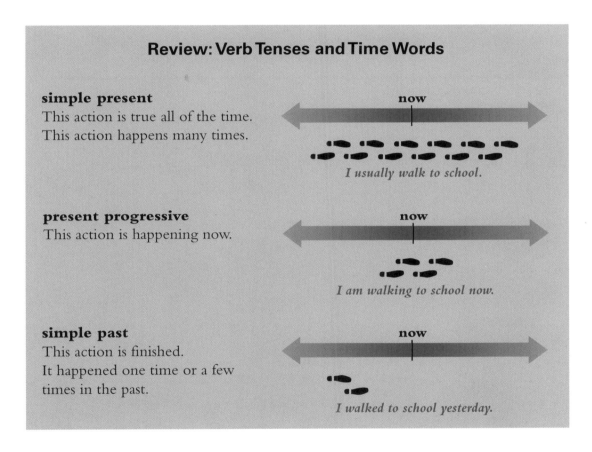

Review: Verb Tenses and Time Words

simple present
This action is true all of the time.
This action happens many times.

I usually walk to school.

present progressive
This action is happening now.

I am walking to school now.

simple past
This action is finished.
It happened one time or a few
times in the past.

I walked to school yesterday.

Exercise 11.   Verb Tenses. Follow the instructions in the box. Then check your answers with a partner.

We use certain verb tenses with certain time words. For example, we use past tense with *last night* and we use simple present with *sometimes*.
Read the list of fifteen time expressions. Put the time expressions with the correct verb tenses. Follow the example.

Simple Present	Simple Past	Present Progressive
every day		

every day	yesterday	this year	last month
sometimes	last night	at this moment	usually
today	all the time	5 minutes ago	this month
in 1993	right now	now	

Exercise 12. Verb Tenses. Write the correct verb forms on the lines.

1. *A:* *(telephone rings)* Hi, Mary? This is Brenda. What _____?
    <u>DO</u>

    B: Nothing special. I _____ the house and _____ to the
       <u>CLEAN</u>   <u>LISTEN</u>
    radio.

    A: Maybe I will go to your house later. Is that OK?

    B: Sure. See you later, then.

2. *(This is a postcard from Greg to his sister Ann.)*

    Dear Ann,

      Hi, hello from Hawaii. I _____ here 2 days ago. On the first day, I
                               <u>ARRIVE</u>
    _____ along the beaches. The weather _____ great. Yester-
       <u>WALK</u>   <u>BE</u>
    day it _____ all day, so I visited a nearby museum. Right now I
           <u>RAIN</u>
    _____ the sunset over the water. It _____ so beautiful. See
       <u>WATCH</u>   <u>BE</u>
    you soon!

                              Love,

                              Greg

3. Susan _____ class every day. She is a good student. Right now she is at
           <u>ATTEND</u>
    the library. She has a test tomorrow, so she _____ because she
                                                   <u>STUDY</u>
    _____ a high grade on the test.
       <u>WANT</u>

Exercise 13.   Verb Tenses. Write the correct verb forms on the lines. Use each verb from the box one time. The numbers before each verb refer to the line where it is located.

1. be	3. live	5. think	7. come	9. mean	11. use
2. own	4. be	6. visit	8. come	10. arrive	12. receive

1   Colorado _____ in the western half of the United States. It ranks eighth in size. It is surrounded by seven states: Kansas, Nebraska, Wyoming, Utah, Arizona, New Mexico, and Oklahoma. The United States government still

2   _____ about one-third of all the land in Colorado.

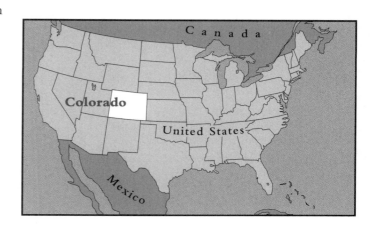

3   Colorado is a large state. Not many people _____ there. The population

4   _____ just over three million. In population, Colorado ranks twenty-eighth and is therefore sort of average, or in the middle, for the fifty states.

5   When people hear the name of this state, they _____ of the natural beauty

6   of Colorado. Thousands of tourists _____ each year. In the summer, they

7   _____ for the beautiful scenery and the mild weather. In the winter, they

8   _____ to enjoy the great skiing.

9   The name Colorado is Spanish. It _____ "colored red." The

10   Spanish people first _____ in Colorado in the 1500s. At that time, they

11   _____ the name Colorado for the river that cuts through the canyons and

12   mountains that are made of red stone. Later the state _____ its name from the river.

Exercise 14.   Multiple Choice. Circle the letter of the correct answer. (Verb
                tenses)

1. "Is Mohamad a good student?"

    "I think he is a very good student. He _____ from 7 to 9 every night."

    (A) is studying   (C) study

    (B) studies   (D) studying

2. "Janice _____ in an apartment."

    "No, that isn't true. Janice lives in a house."

    (A) lived   (C) live

    (B) lives   (D) was live

3. "This test is the last test. I am so happy!"

    "Me, too! I _____ tests!"

    (A) don't like   (C) didn't like

    (B) am not liking   (D) am not like

4. "How many dictionaries _____ now?"

    "Three. One is English-English, and the others are French-English."

    (A) are you owning   (C) own you

    (B) do you own   (D) you own

5. *Jim:*   "Did the students in your class buy a present for your teacher?"

    Todd: "Yes, we did."

    Jim: "What did the students buy?"

    Todd: "Well, Mark and I _____ to buy a new watch, but the other students said no.

               They said a new shirt was the best gift."

    (A) want   (C) wanted

    (B) are wanting   (D) are going to want

6. "Let's go to the beach tomorrow. It's Saturday."

    "I can't. Every Saturday I _____ with Fran at the library."

    (A) am studying   (C) studied

    (B) am study   (D) study

7. "How was the test?"

   "I _____ it. My score was 83."

   (A) pass   (C) am going to pass

   (B) am passing   (D) passed

8. "How do you like your new class?"

   "It isn't bad, but it's difficult for me to arrive on time. I usually _____ up so late."

   (A) waking   (C) wake

   (B) am going to wake   (D) am waking

─────

Exercise 15.   Prepositions: *at, on, in.* Write the correct prepositions on the lines.

1. *A:* Where do you live?

   B: I live _____ an apartment _____ Goode Street.

   A: Really, I live near that area. What's the name of the complex?

   B: Hillside Manor. Do you know it?

   A: No, I don't.

   B: Well, it's _____ Goode Street between the post office and Union Bank.

2. *A:* When did you arrive _____ the U.S.?

   B: _____ March of last year.

   A: When will you go back to your country?

   B: Probably _____ December.

3. *A:* When is the next TOEFL?

   B: It's _____ Saturday.

   A: You mean it's _____ May 8?

   B: Yes, that's right.

   A: Where is it?

   B: The test will be _____ room 207 _____ Cooper Hall.

4. *A:* Where does your cat sleep?

   B: It sleeps _____ a box _____ the closet _____ my bedroom.

   A: So it sleeps _____ the house then?

   B: Yes, that's right.

Appendix of Irregular Verbs

List of 78 Irregular Past Tense Verbs

Present	Past	Present	Past	Present	Past
become	became	go	went	sell	sold
begin	began	grow	grew	send	sent
bite	bit	hang	hung	set	set
blow	blew	have	had	shoot	shot
break	broke	hear	heard	shut	shut
bring	brought	hide	hid	sing	sang
build	built	hold	held	sit	sat
buy	bought	hurt	hurt	sleep	slept
catch	caught	keep	kept	speak	spoke
choose	chose	know	knew	spend	spent
come	came	lead	led	spread	spread
cost	cost	leave	left	stand	stood
cut	cut	lend	lent	steal	stole
do	did	let	let	stick	stuck
draw	drew	lie★	lay	swim	swam
drink	drank	lose	lost	take	took
drive	drove	make	made	teach	taught
eat	ate	mean	meant	tear	tore
fall	fell	meet	met	tell	told
feel	felt	put	put	think	thought
fight	fought	read	read	throw	threw
find	found	ride	rode	understand	understood
fly	flew	ring	rang	wake	woke
forget	forget	run	ran	wear	wore
get	got	say	said	win	won
give	gave	see	saw	write	wrote

★lie = lie down (recline); not tell the truth = lie, lied

Answer Key

Pre-Unit

Ex. 1, p. 1: 1. John, Mark, apartment, Miami 2. color, car, red 3. Mr. Jenks, teacher, class 4. chair, window 5. weather 6. car 7. tennis, park, Monday 8. books, desk, row 9. bus, station 10. library, school, lake

Ex. 2, p. 2: 1. live 2. is 3. is, teaches 4. sit 5. was 6. is 7. played, 's (or is) 8. is 9. drives, 's (or is) 10. don't like, give

Ex. 3, p. 2: 1. small 2. best, new 3. my, second 4. (none) 5. summer, hot, humid 6. big, beautiful, big 7. difficult 8. teacher's, brown 9. old, five, large 10. large, old, small, quiet

Ex. 4, p. 3: 1. n 2. v 3. adj 4. n 5. v 6. n 7. v 8. v 9. n 10. adj 11. n 12. adj 13. n 14. v 15. adj 16. n 17. v 18. adj 19. n 20. v

Unit 1

Ex. 1, p. 7: 1. am 2. are 3. is 4. is 5. is 6. are 7. are 8. are

Ex. 2, p. 7: 1. is, is 2. are, is 3. are, is, is, are 4. is, are, is 5. am, is, is, are, is, is

Ex. 3, p. 8: 1. is 2. is 3. are 4. is 5. are 6. is, is 7. is 8. is 9. are, am 10. are 11. is 12. am 13. are 14. is 15. are 16. are 17. am 18. are 19. is 20. is

Ex. 4, p. 8: 1. are, is, is 2. is, is 3. is, is, are 4. is, is, is 5. is, is, are, is, am 6. is, is, is, are

Ex. 5, p. 9: 1. X (reading = is reading) 2. X (are = is) 3. C 4. C 5. X (Anthea = is Anthea) 6. X (are = is) 7. X (between = is between) 8. C 9. C 10. C

Ex. 6, p. 10: Student A: you are, the girl is, the cat is, today is, Eric is, Joe and Pam are, my car is, the boys are, dinner is, Toronto is; Student B: he is, Rachel is, the cats are, we are, the shoes are, the teacher is, Brazil is, the boy is, I am, the weather is

Ex. 7, p. 10: 1. am 2. are 3. are 4. are 5. is 6. is 7. am 8. is 9. are 10. are 11. is 12. am

Ex. 8, p. 13: 1. D isn't, J isn't 2. Dennis isn't, Marsha isn't 3. orange isn't 4. cat isn't, go and stop aren't

Ex. 9, p. 13: 1. isn't, is, is 2. am not, am 3. isn't, are 4. are, is, isn't 5. isn't, is, are, aren't, are 6. aren't, are

Ex. 10, p. 14: Student A: lunch isn't, my friends aren't, today isn't, Peter isn't, you aren't, the child isn't, the cat isn't, my parents aren't, Ben and Ted aren't, the birds aren't; Student B: I am not, the weather isn't, we aren't, my shoes aren't, he isn't, Katie isn't, Japan isn't, my brother isn't, the teacher isn't, my car isn't

Ex. 11, p. 15: 1. Is it a good book? 2. Is the movie good? 3. Are they from Italy? 4. Are they in the same class? 5. Is she in the hospital again? 6. Is she all right? 7. Is she really sick? 8. Is there a flight on Monday? 9. Is it in the morning? 10. Is the flight full?

Ex. 12, p. 16: 1. Is Mrs. Smith happy today? 2. Are the cats thirsty now? 3. Are Paul and Naomi in class today? 4. Is the weather cold now? 5. Is his homework correct? 6. Are you late to class every day? 7. Is Caracas the capital of Venezuela? 8. Is the bank on Ben Street open now? 9. Is the park crowded on Saturday? 10. Are Sam and Vick sleepy today? 11. Is the teacher very busy now? 12. Is Robert early to class every day?

Ex. 13, p. 17: 1. Is, —, is 2. Is, —, isn't, is, am 3. Is, —, is, am, is 4. Are, —, is 5. Are, —, am 6. Are, —, aren't, are

Ex. 14, p. 18: 1. Yes, they are. No, they aren't. 2. Yes, they are. No, they aren't. 3. Yes, I am. No, I am not. (or Yes, we are. No, we aren't.) 4. Yes, it is. No, it isn't. 5. Yes, we are. No, we aren't. 6. Yes, it is. No, it isn't. 7. Yes, he (she) is. No, he (she) isn't. 8. Yes, they are. No, they aren't. 9. Yes, it is. No, it isn't. 10. Yes, he is. No, he isn't.

Ex. 16, p. 20: 1. B 2. C 3. B 4. A 5. C 6. B 7. C 8. D

Ex. 17, p. 21: Part 1. 1st paragraph: is, is, is, is, is; 2nd paragraph: are, is, is; 3rd paragraph: is, are, is, are, is, is; Part 2. ten = is ten, Is = He is, name Jenny = name is Jenny, She in = She is in, school elementary = elementary school, Chris and Jenny is = Chris and Jenny are; Part 3. 1. correct 2. wrong (Miss Miller is) 3. correct 4. correct 5. wrong (price is) 6. wrong (no are = aren't) 7. correct

Unit 2

Ex. 1, p. 26: he, she, it, Jo = speaks, watches, does, tries, takes, plays, has; all others = speak, watch, do, try, take, play, have; *Be:* I am, he/she/it/Jo = is; all others = are

Ex. 2, p. 27: 1. plays, plays, enjoy 2. do, make, makes, uses 3. work, works, works, work 4. tries, likes 5. begins, arrives, come, likes, comes, gets 6. works, finishes, goes, watches, eats, comes, watch

Ex. 3, p. 27: 1. play 2. has 3. speaks 4. takes 5. need 6. come 7. drinks 8. drink 9. explains 10. ask 11. answers 12. is

Ex. 4, p. 28: (answers may vary) 1. have, are 2. watch, watches, has, is, have, is 3. is, studies, does, is 4. help, helps 5. is, swims 6. live, like, has, are, is, watch 7. works, is, teaches, lives, leaves, drives, takes, arrives, begins (or is)

Ex. 5, p. 29: answers will vary

Ex. 6, p. 31: he, she, it, Jo = doesn't like, doesn't go, doesn't do, doesn't study, doesn't know, doesn't get, doesn't have; all others = don't like, don't go, don't do, don't study, don't know, don't get, don't have; *be* = I am not, he/she/it/Jo isn't, all others aren't

Ex. 7, p. 32: 1. don't 2. doesn't 3. don't 4. don't 5. don't 6. don't 7. don't 8. don't 9. doesn't 10. doesn't 11. don't 12. doesn't

Ex. 8, p. 33: 1. don't go 2. don't drink 3. doesn't have 4. doesn't speak 5. doesn't take 6. doesn't study 7. don't read 8. don't do 9. doesn't swim 10. don't teach 11. doesn't begin 12. don't play

Ex. 9, p. 33: 1. doesn't like, doesn't like, doesn't have 2. isn't, doesn't have, doesn't have 3. don't do, don't know 4. doesn't have, doesn't cook 5. don't live, don't walk 6. doesn't have, isn't, doesn't take

Ex. 10, p. 34: answers will vary

Ex. 11, p. 36: 1. Do 2. Does, Do, Do 3. Does 4. Do 5. Do 6. Do

Ex. 12, p. 36: 1. Does, have 2. Do, play 3. Does, rain 4. Does, study 5. Do, want 6. Do, read 7. Do, take 8. Do, drive 9. Does, cook 10. Do, speak 11. Do, have 12. Does, go

Ex. 13, p. 37: 1. Do, eat, I don't eat, I eat 2. Does, go, she doesn't go, She goes 3. Does, do, he doesn't do, He does 4. Does, have, it doesn't have, It has 5. Do, speak, they don't speak, They speak

Ex. 14, p. 37: 1. Does your telephone have a fax? 2. Does a police officer wear blue jeans? 3. Do police in England have guns? 4. Do you and your family live in a very old house? 5. Does it get very cold in the winter? 6. Do Mr. and Mrs. Caruthers have many children? 7. Do banks open on Sundays? 8. Do I eat too much? 9. Does a cheeseburger cost one dollar?

Ex. 15, p. 39: 1. Yes, they do./No, they don't. 2. Yes, it does./No, it doesn't. 3. Yes, he does./No, he doesn't. 4. Yes, we do./No, we don't. 5. Yes, it does./No, it doesn't. 6. Yes, you do./No, you don't. 7. Yes, he (she) does./No, he (she) doesn't. 8. Yes, it does./No, it doesn't.

Ex. 16, p. 40: answers will vary

Ex. 17, p. 40: 1. A 2. C 3. B 4. D 5. A 6. D 7. B 8. D

Ex. 18, p. 41: Part 1. 1st paragraph: don't, isn't, don't, isn't, aren't; 2nd paragraph: don't, doesn't, isn't; 3rd paragraph: doesn't, don't, doesn't, isn't; Part 2. doesn't = isn't, don't = aren't, no are = aren't, aren't = don't, doesn't = don't; Part 3. 1. wrong (isn't) 2. correct 3. wrong (doesn't have) 4. wrong (doesn't speak) 5. correct 6. wrong (aren't)

Unit 3

Ex. 1, p. 44: 1. this 2. these 3. this 4. this 5. this 6. these 7. these 8. these 9. this 10. these 11. that 12. those 13. that 14. those 15. that 16. that 17. those 18. those 19. those 20. that

Ex. 2, p. 45: 1. These 2. this 3. Those 4. this 5. That 6. this 7. those 8. this 9. Those 10. those 11. This 12. Those 13. Those 14. Those 15. this

Ex. 3, p. 46: 1. This diamond 2. These diamonds 3. This test 4. These tests 5. These cheeseburgers 6. That trip 7. Those tables 8. That table 9. Those sandwiches 10. That sandwich

Ex. 4, p. 46: that, That, that, this, that, those, These, These, those

Ex. 5, p. 47: answers will vary

Ex. 6, p. 48: 1. D 2. C 3. D 4. A 5. B 6. A 7. B 8. A

Ex. 7, p. 49: Part 1. that, That, that, that, this, that; Part 2. 1. wrong (shirts) 2. wrong (this) 3. wrong (that) 4. correct 5. wrong (Those) 6. correct 7. correct

Unit 4

Ex. 1, p. 53: 1. your 2. her 3. your 4. her 5. our 6. its 7. their 8. its 9. their 10. its 11. our 12. his 13. his 14. her 15. her 16. their 17. their 18. our 19. their 20. our

Challenge, p. 53: Only #12 is correct. Singular (test) or plural (tests) doesn't make any difference here. Use *his* with *he.*

Ex. 2, p. 53: 1. my 2. his 3. our 4. her 5. his 6. your 7. its 8. its 9. his 10. their 11. her 12. our 13. our 14. its 15. his 16. her 17. their 18. their 19. their 20. their 21. our 22. his 23. your 24. his 25. his 26. her 27. her 28. her 29. our 30. her or his

Challenge, p. 54: There are two boys, so we use *their. His* is singular.

Ex. 3, p. 54: 1. my 2. his 3. Their 4. your 5. her 6. Our 7. our 8. His 9. Its 10. My

Ex. 4, p. 54: 1. your, your, My, your, His, his, my, My 2. My, your, My, his, their, Their, my, their

Ex. 5, p. 56: 1. I 2. his 3. Their 4. They 5. She, her 6. We, our 7. We 8. He, He 9. It 10. you

Ex. 6, p. 56: 1. C 2. X (your = you) 3. X (it = its) 4. X (she sister = her sister) 5. C 6. X (I first = my first) 7. C 8. X (His = He) 9. X (we favorite = our favorite) 10. X (Their = They) 11. X (They = Their) 12. C

Ex. 7, p. 56: answers will vary

Ex. 8, p. 58: 1. B 2. C 3. A 4. B 5. C 6. D 7. C 8. C

Ex. 9, p. 58: Part 1. 1. their 2. his 3. Their 4. your 5. I 6. Our 7. our 8. His 9. Its 10. His; Part 2. 1st paragraph: my, my, Her; 2nd paragraph: my, His, his, Her; 3rd paragraph: Their, their, Its; Part 3. 1. wrong (she = her) 2. correct 3. correct 4. wrong (they're = their) 5. correct 6. correct 7. correct

Unit 5

Ex. 1, p. 61: 1. was 2. was 3. was 4. was 5. were 6. was, was 7. was 8. was 9. were 10. were

Ex. 2, p. 62: 1. am 2. was 3. were 4. were 5. was 6. is 7. was 8. was 9. was 10. were 11. was 12. is

Ex. 3, p. 62: 1. was = is, is = was, is = was 2. is = was, is = was, is = was, is = was 3. is = was, is = was, is = was

Ex. 4, p. 63: Student A: you were, the girl was, the cat was, yesterday was, Peter was, Joe and Pam were, my car was, the boys were, dinner was, they were; Student B: he was, Rachel was, the cats were, we were, the shoes were, the teacher was, Brazil was, the boy was, I was, the weather was

Ex. 5, p. 65: 1. wasn't 2. wasn't, wasn't 3. weren't 4. wasn't 5. wasn't 6. wasn't 7. wasn't 8. weren't 9. wasn't 10. wasn't

Ex. 6, p. 65: Student A: lunch wasn't, my friends weren't, yesterday wasn't, Peter wasn't, you weren't, the child wasn't, the cat wasn't, my parents weren't, Ben and Ted weren't, the birds weren't; Student B: I wasn't, the weather wasn't, we weren't, my shoes weren't, he wasn't, Andy wasn't, Japan wasn't, my brother wasn't, the teacher wasn't, my car wasn't

Ex. 7, p. 67: 1. Was Mrs. Smith happy yesterday? 2. Were the cats thirsty yesterday? 3. Were Paul and Naomi in class yesterday? 4. Was the weather cold yesterday? 5. Was his homework correct yesterday? 6. Were you late to class yesterday? 7. Was the kitchen dirty yesterday? 8. Was the store open yesterday? 9. Was the park crowded yesterday? 10. Were Sam and Vick sleepy yesterday? 11. Was the teacher busy yesterday? 12. Was Robert early yesterday?

Ex. 8, p. 67: (answers may vary) 1. Was the teacher tired after class? 2. Was the weather really hot? 3. Was the flight from Vancouver late by 15 minutes? 4. Was the movie better than the book? 5. Was your dinner delicious? 6. Was the baby born at General Hospital? 7. Were Sandra and Kevin in the same class last year? 8. Were her parents students at the same high school? 9. Were the kittens hungry?

Ex. 9, p. 69: 1. Yes, it was./No, it wasn't. 2. Yes, they were./No, they weren't. 3. Yes, I was./No, I wasn't. 4. Yes, it was./No, it wasn't. 5. Yes, we were./No, we weren't. 6. Yes, it was./No, it wasn't. 7. Yes, he (she) was./No, he (she) wasn't. 8. Yes, they were./No, they weren't. 9. Yes, it was./No, it wasn't. 10. Yes, she was./No, she wasn't.

Ex. 10, p. 70: answers will vary

Ex. 11, p. 70: 1. B 2. A 3. B 4. B 5. C 6. A 7. D 8. A

Ex. 12, p. 72: Part 1. was, were, was, was (or wasn't), was; Part 2. am = was, is = was, are = were, is = was, is = was; Part 3. 1. correct 2. wrong (am = was) 3. wrong (is = was) 4. wrong (was = were) 5. correct 6. correct 7. correct

Unit 6

Ex. 1, p. 75: 1, 2. work 3, 4, 5. works 6, 7. work 8.–14. worked 15. every day, at night, all of the time, most of the time, every afternoon 16. yesterday, last night, an hour ago, last week, in 1993

Ex. 2, p. 76: (for all subjects) learned, liked, watched, washed, chopped, watched, practiced, tried, studied, listened, played, repeated

Ex. 3, p. 77: 1. wanted 2. attended 3. repeated 4. talked 5. needed 6. repeated 7. counted 8. typed 9. watched 10. shouted 11. listened 12. waited 13. learned 14. explained 15. used 16. liked 17. added 18. shopped 19. studied 20. answered

Ex. 4, p. 78: 1. walked 2. listened 3. cleaned 4. answered 5. needed 6. coughed 7. rained 8. presented 9. introduced 10. shouted

Ex. 5, p. 78: A. d B. Id C. Id D. t E. t F. d G. d H. Id I. t J. d K. d L. M. d N. t O. Id; 1. erased 2. robbed 3. sneezed 4. signed 5. cooked 6. washed, ironed, folded 7. carried 8. helped 9. needed 10. failed 11. passed 12. waited 13. counted

Ex. 6, p. 79: 1. plays, rained, played, was 2. is, opened 3. like, loves 4. like, tries, cooked, was, was 5. cleaned, washed, planted, played 6. call, called 7. work, works, works, work 8. plays, watched

Ex. 7, p. 80: 1. watched, arrived, watched, started, finished 2. cooked, was, washed, cleaned 3. wanted, called, asked, wanted, walked, studied 4. explained, asked, answered

Ex. 8, p. 82: 1. I want, I don't want, I wanted, I didn't want 2. he listens, he doesn't listen, he listened, he didn't listen 3. they learn, they don't learn, they learned, they didn't learn 4. Bill likes, Bill doesn't like, Bill liked, Bill didn't like 5. we watch, we don't watch, we watched, we didn't watch 6. you practice, you don't practice, you practiced, you didn't practice 7. he studies, he doesn't study, he studied, he didn't study 8. I play, I don't play, I played, I didn't play 9. it repeats, it doesn't repeat, it repeated, it didn't repeat 10. they shop, they don't shop, they shopped, they didn't shop 11. we mail, we don't mail, we mailed, we didn't mail 12. he explains, he doesn't explain, he explained, he didn't explain 13. I answer, I don't answer, I answered, I didn't answer 14. she chops, she doesn't chop, she chopped, she didn't chop 15. we erase, we don't erase, we erased, we didn't erase

Ex. 9, p. 83: answers will vary

Ex. 10, p. 84: 1. Did 2. wait 3. Did 4. count 5. use 6. Did 7. snore 8. present

Ex. 11, p. 85: 1. Did, dream, I didn't dream, I dreamed (OR dreamt) 2. Did, fail, she didn't fail, She failed 3. Did, visit, he didn't visit, He visited 4. Did, laugh, I didn't laugh, laughed 5. Did, lock, he didn't lock, locked

Ex. 12, p. 86: 1. Yes, I did./No, I didn't. 2. Yes, it did./No, it didn't. 3. Yes, they did./No, they didn't. 4. Yes, we did./No, we didn't. 5. Yes, it did./No, it didn't.

Ex. 13, p. 87: answers will vary

Ex. 14, p. 89: 1. drank 2. gave 3. told 4. read 5. began 6. got 7. saw 8. bought 9. took 10. went 11. sent 12. ate 13. had 14. made 15. spoke 16. forgot 17. put 18. came 19. wrote 20. chose

Ex. 15, p. 90: answers will vary

Ex. 16, p. 90: 1. we begin, we don't begin, we didn't begin, Do we begin, Did we begin 2. she gets, she got, she doesn't get, Does she get, Did she get 3. I wake, I woke, I didn't wake, Do I wake, Did I wake 4. you sell, you sold, you don't sell, you didn't sell, Did you sell 5. you think, you thought, you don't think, you didn't think, Do you think 6. it took, it doesn't take, it didn't take, Does it take, Did it take 7. he speaks, he doesn't speak, he didn't speak, Does he speak, Did he speak 8. I make, I made, I don't make, I didn't make, Did I make 9. he has, he had, he doesn't have, Does he have, Did he have 10. she puts, she put, she doesn't put, Does she put, Did she put

Ex. 17, p. 91: 1. gave 2. come 3. took 4. forget 5. left 6. were 7. began 8. do 9. ate 10. get

Ex. 18, p. 91: answers will vary

Ex. 19, p. 92: answers will vary

Ex. 20, p. 94: Student A: went, woke, ate, lost, told, sent, bought; Student B: made, got, went, spent, understood, slept, had

Ex. 21, p. 95: 1. A 2. B 3. C 4. D 5. D 6. D 7. C 8. A

Ex. 22, p. 96: Part 1. 1. go, is, watch, watched, liked, didn't like, was 2. cooked, was, tasted, washed, cleaned 3. like, explains, writes, answers, explained, studied; Part 2. 1. correct 2. wrong (cried) 3. correct 4. correct 5. wrong (Did you work) 6. wrong (made) 7. wrong (didn't) 8. correct

Unit 7

Ex. 1, p. 99: 1. When 2. Who 3. Why 4. What 5. When 6. What 7. What 8. Where 9. Which 10. Who

Ex. 2, p. 99: 1. Does Paul read mystery stories on the weekend? Yes, he does./No, he doesn't. What does Paul read on the weekend? Mystery stories. 2. Is Tina a dentist? Yes, she is./No, she isn't. What is Tina? A dentist. 3. Did Victor study French with Mark? Yes, he did./No, he didn't. What did Victor study with Mark? French. 4. Do you like tennis and football? Yes, I do./No, I don't. (or Yes, we do./No, we don't.) What do you like? Tennis and football.

Ex. 3, p. 100: 1. Did Victor begin the work at 10 A.M.? Yes, he did./No, he didn't. When did Victor begin the work? At 10 A.M. 2. Do the girls watch a movie every Friday night? Yes, they do./No, they don't. When do the girls watch a movie? Every Friday night. 3. Was the big tennis tournament last weekend? Yes, it was./No, it wasn't. When was the big tennis tournament? Last weekend. 4. Does Laura take a long walk every Sunday morning? Yes, she does./No, she doesn't. When does Laura take a long walk? Every Sunday morning.

Ex. 4, p. 101: 1. Do you live on Green Street? Yes, I do./No, I don't. (or Yes, we do./No, we don't.) Where do you live? On Green Street. 2. Did they watch a movie at Carl's house? Yes, they did./No, they didn't. Where did they watch a movie? At Carl's house. 3. Do Zina and Ellen work at the bakery? Yes, they do./No, they don't. Where do Zina and Ellen work? At the bakery. 4. Were the books in the desk drawer? Yes, they were./No, they weren't. Where were the books? In the desk drawer.

Ex. 5, p. 102: 1. Does Victor speak French because he lived in France? Yes, he does./No, he doesn't. Why does Victor speak French? Because he lived in France. 2. Did Mark stay home because it was too cold to go outside? Yes, he did./No, he didn't. Why did Mark stay home? Because it was too cold to go outside. 3. Do you like volleyball because it has a lot of quick points? Yes, I do./No, I don't. (or Yes, we do./No, we don't.) Why do you like volleyball? Because it has a lot of quick points. 4. Is Tina a teacher because she likes children? Yes, she is./No, she isn't. Why is Tina a teacher? Because she likes children.

Ex. 6, p. 103: 1. Which bread is on sale? The bread on the top shelf. 2. Which question was the most difficult? Question number seven. 3. Which class do you like the best? Grammar class. 4. Which flowers come from Mexico? Those white flowers. 5. Of all the restaurants, which does he like the best? McDonald's.

Ex. 7, p. 104: 1. Who is their grammar teacher? Mr. Miller. 2. Who helped Alan with the homework? Joe. 3. Who waited for Tom? Pam and Bob. 4. Who is a dentist? Mrs. Yates. 5. Who talked to Pat? Wendy.

Ex. 8, p. 105: 1. understands 2. has 3. lives 4. drives 5. was 6. is (teacher) 7. are (friends) 8. are (singers) 9. was (teacher) 10. is (he)

Ex. 9, p. 106: 1. understands 2. are (actors) 3. drives 4. was 5. is (teacher) 6. are (teachers) 7. has 8. lives 9. was (uncle) 10. is (she) 11. wants 12. is 13. are (parents) 14. are (cousins) 15. lives 16. are (Bill and Hillary Clinton) 17. goes 18. has 19. plays 20. studies

Ex. 10, p. 107: 1. Who 2. Whom 3. Who 4. Whom 5. Who 6. Who 7. Whom 8. Who 9. Who 10. Who 11. Whom 12. Who

Ex. 11, p. 108: 1. Whom 2. Who 3. Whom 4. Who 5. Whom 6. Who 7. Whom 8. Who 9. Who 10. Who 11. Who 12. Who

Ex. 12, p. 108: 1. Who visited Martha yesterday? Whom did Jane visit yesterday? 2. Who studies with Matt? Whom does Ann study with? 3. Who studies with Matt in the evening? Whom do Ann and Bob study with in the evening? 4. Who plays tennis with Anne and Matt every day? Whom do John and Martha play tennis with every day? 5. Who waited for all the students? Whom did the teacher wait for? 6. Who knows Jack well? Whom does Ted know well? 7. Who telephoned Keith? Whom did Carlos telephone? 8. Who has a class with Danny? Whom does Jan have a class with?

Ex. 13, p. 110: 1. What does hard mean? It means difficult (or not soft). 2. What does sour mean? It means not sweet. 3. What does quantity mean? It means how much (or the number of something). 4. What does a few mean? It means not many (or a small number of something). 5, 6. answers will vary

Ex. 14, p. 110: 1. When does she arrive? 2. Where did Mary learn French? 3. Who(m) did she ask? 4. Who wants a new car? 5. What does Jane have? 6. Where are the boys? 7. Who is in the kitchen?

8. Where do they go every summer? 9. When do they go to Florida? 10. Who/m did you play tennis with? 11. Why does Yuri walk to school? 12. What does fiesta mean?

Ex. 15, p. 111: 1. A. Who studied French with Paul and Sue last night? B. What did Mary study with Paul and Sue last night? C. Who(m) did Mary study French with last night? D. When did Mary study French with Paul and Sue? 2. What does hilarious mean? 3. A. Who listens to the radio every night? B. Why do they do this? 4. A. Who invented the lightbulb? B. What did Thomas Edison invent? C. Where was he born? D. When did he die?

Ex. 16, p. 112: Conversation 1. Person A: 1, 5, 7, 11, 3, 13, 9; Person B: 4, 10, 6, 14, 8, 12, 2; Conversation 2. Person A: 1, 3, 13, 7, 9, 11, 5, 15; Person B: 4, 16, 12, 14, 2, 6, 8, 10; Conversation 3. Person A: 1, 11, 7, 5, 3, 9; Person B: 4, 6, 8, 2, 10, 12

Ex. 17, p. 113:

Name	St. No.	Country	Born	Arrived/U.S.	Teacher
Susan Johnson	228441	Sweden	Stockholm	January 1995	Mr. Green
Katrina Gomez	228497	Peru	Lima	last year	Mr. Benson
Brian Andros	219558	Greece	Athens	March 1995	Ms. Jody
Paul Lee	223819	Taiwan	Taipei	two years ago	Mr. Mills
Emi Tanaka	228114	Japan	Tokyo	last October	Ms. Valen

Ex. 18, p. 114: 1. C 2. D 3. A 4. C 5. B (D is OK for students who have not studied *whom*.) 6. B 7. D 8. A

Ex. 19, p. 116: Part 1. 1. Where 2. are 3. Why 4. What 5. When 6. does pink mean 7. has 8. do you study; Part 2. 1. wrong (When was) 2. wrong (What does this word mean?) 3. correct 4. wrong (Why do you study English in America?) 5. correct 6. wrong (What does Victor have); Part 3. 1. Whom 2. Who 3. Who 4. Who 5. Who 6. Who

Unit 8

Ex. 1, p. 119: 1. place 2. time 3. time 4. place 5. time 6. time 7. place 8. time 9. place 10. time

Ex. 2, p. 120: 1. We eat lunch in a restaurant at noon. 2. They have class at the university at 10 A.M. 3. I have coffee there before class. 4. He studies French and math in the library every night. 5. She practices pronunciation in the laboratory every day. 6. They go to class every day. 7. You drink milk at the table in the morning. 8. You write letters in the library at night. 9. She studies in class every day. 10. He comes to class every afternoon. 11. We eat lunch at a small table in the Chinese restaurant on Green Street. 12. She practices pronunciation in the laboratory from 2 to 3 on Mondays. 13. Mr. Miller prefers to sit in an aisle seat in first class on a 747. 14. Three of four Canadians live within one hundred miles of the U.S. border.

Ex. 3, p. 121: answers will vary

Ex. 4, p. 122: 1. your first class, easy, difficult class 2. my favorite professor, intelligent 3. big cheese sandwiches, American cheese, Swiss cheese, yellow cheese 4. most important people

Ex. 5, p. 123: 1. D 2. C 3. C 4. C 5. A 6. B 7. D 8. B

Ex. 6, p. 124: Part 1. On Pine Street she lives = She lives on Pine Street, house white = white house, in 1959 born in this house = born in this house in 1959, things differents = different things, behind her house every morning in the small garden = in the small garden behind her house every morning; Part 2. 1. We lived in a small house on Green Street last year. 2. Most students arrive at school before nine. 3. The next meeting will take place in room 105 at 8 P.M. on March 7th. 4. Our teacher and his family traveled from Ontario to Nova Scotia; Part 3. 1. correct 2. wrong (at John's party at 7 P.M. on Wednesday night) 3. correct 4. wrong (here at noon) 5. correct 6. correct 7. wrong (in the top drawer in Mike's desk)

Unit 9

grammar rule, p. 127: We use present progressive for actions that are now, right now, or this ____ (this week, this month, this year). We use simple present with things that are usually or always true.

Ex. 1, p. 130: 1, 2. work 3, 4, 5. works 6, 7. work 8. am working 9. are working 10, 11, 12. is working 13, 14. are working 15. 1, 4, 7. every day 2. at night 3. all of the time 5. most of the time 6. every afternoon 8, 12, 14. now 9. right now 10. today 11. this week 13. this semester

Ex. 2, p. 131: I am (counting, taking, drinking, running), you/we/they/Jo and I are (counting, taking, drinking, running), he/she/it/Jo is (counting, taking, drinking, running)

Ex. 3, p. 132: 1. you are reading 2. X 3. you are repeating 4. we are asking 5. we are going 6. X 7. I am counting 8. they are typing 9. I am watching 10. you are shouting 11. she is listening 12. I am waiting 13. he is learning

14. they are explaining 15. she is using 16. X 17. X 18. I am shopping 19. X 20. he is taking

Ex. 4, p. 132: 1. read 2. am reading 3. is studying 4. studies 5. play 6. is playing 7. likes 8. likes 9. have 10. are having 11. am cooking 12. cook

Ex. 5, p. 133: you (S)/are doing (V), things (S)/are (V), I (S)/hope (V), everything (S)/is going (V), I (S)/'m writing (V), I (S)/want (V), I (S)/have (V), I (S)/have (V), you (S)/do remember (V), it (S)/wasn't (V), rent (S)/was (V), I (S)/decided (V), address (S)/is (V), city (S)/is (V), you (S)/are working (V), your boss (S)/is (V), you (S)/can say (V), I (S)/talked (V), I (S)/visited (V), he (S)/'s (V), I (S)/'m going (V), it (S)/'s (V), I (S)/have (V)

Ex. 6, p. 134: 1. Are Mark and Joe studying English together? Yes, they are. 2. Am I sitting in your chair? Yes, you are. 3. Is it snowing now? Yes, it is. 4. Is Victor watching football on TV? No, he isn't. 5. Is the teacher talking about the homework? Yes, he (she) is.

Ex. 7, p. 135: 1 A. Does Jill swim five laps every day? B. Is Jill swimming in the pool now? 2 A. Does Mr. Yoshida teach history? B. Is Mr. Yoshida teaching Sue now? 3 A. Are they having a good time there? B. Do they have a good time in that class? 4 A. Is it snowing heavily now? B. Does it snow a lot in January? 5 A. Does Joshua take a shower at night? B. Is Joshua taking a shower now? 6 A. Is Mr. Po preparing lunch? B. Does Mr. Po prepare lunch every day? 7 A. Are Henry and Mark studying? B. Do Henry and Mark study together? 8 A. Are you playing a match now? B. Do you play tennis very well?

Ex. 8, p. 135: 1 A. Yes, she does. B. No, she isn't. 2 A. No, he doesn't. B. No, he isn't. 3 A. Yes, they are. B. Yes, they do. 4 A. No, it isn't. B. Yes, it does. 5 A. Yes, he does. B. No, he isn't. 6 A. Yes, he is. B. Yes, he does. 7 A. No, they aren't. B. Yes, they do. 8 A. No, I am not. (or No, we aren't.) B. Yes, I do. (or Yes, we do.)

Ex. 9, p. 136: 1. are you cooking 2. are you playing 3. are you hurrying 4. are you calling 5. are you going

Ex. 10, p. 137: 1. I work, I don't work, I am working, I am not working 2. he likes, he doesn't like, X, X 3. they want, they don't want, X, X 4. Bill listens, Bill doesn't listen, Bill is listening, Bill isn't listening 5. we watch, we don't watch, we are watching, we aren't watching 6. you practice, you don't practice, you are practicing, you aren't practicing 7. he is, he isn't, X, X 8. I play, I don't play, I am playing, I am not playing 9. it begins, it doesn't begin, it is beginning, it isn't beginning 10. they sing, they don't sing, they are singing, they aren't singing 11. we know, we don't know,

X, X 12. he explains, he doesn't explain, he is explaining, he isn't explaining 13. I answer, I don't answer, I am answering, I am not answering 14. she prefers, she doesn't prefer, X, X 15. we understand, we don't understand, X, X

Ex. 11, p. 138: answers will vary

Ex. 12, p. 139: 1. B 2. B 3. C 4. C 5. A 6. D 7. D 8. A

Ex. 13, p. 140: Part 1. 1. is 2. is shining 3. has 4. is sitting 5. is sleeping 6. are playing 7. are smiling 8. is eating 9. is drinking 10. doesn't like 11. is flying 12. is blowing; Part 2. 1. wrong ('s watching) 2. wrong (Is Linda going) 3. correct 4. wrong (aren't doing) 5. correct

Unit 10

Ex. 1, p. 144: 1. C 2. C 3. NC 4. C 5. NC 6. NC 7. C 8. NC 9. NC 10. C 11. C 12. NC 13. C 14. NC 15. C

Ex. 2, p. 144: 1. a 2. a 3. a 4. a 5. some 6. a 7. a 8. some 9. some 10. some 11. a 12. some 13. a 14. some 15. a 16. a 17. a 18. a 19. some 20. a

Ex. 3, p. 145: (numbers may vary) 1. some 2. 3 shirts 3. some 4. 20 flights 5. 2 engines 6. some 7. some trucks 8. some 9. 12 eggs 10. 4 problems 11. some 12. some 13. 100 jars 14. some 15. 2 parents 16. some 17. 2 shoes 18. 7 facts 19. 3 suits 20. 5 trips

Ex. 4, p. 145: 1. some, some, a 2. a, some, an, some, a, an, some, some 3. a, some some, an 4. some, some, some 5. some, some, a, an, some

Ex. 5, p. 146: answers will vary

Ex. 6, p. 148: 1. some, some 2. some or any, any 3. some or any, some or any 4. some or any, any, some 5. any, any

Ex. 7, p. 149: 1. some, any, some 2. some, any 3. some/any, some, any 4. some, any, some, some, some, some, some/any

Ex. 8, p. 151: 1. many, a lot of 2. a lot of 3. much, a lot of 4. much, a lot of 5. much, a lot of 6. Many, A lot of 7. a lot of 8. many, a lot of 9. many, a lot of 10. much, a lot of 11. many, a lot of 12. much, a lot of 13. a lot of 14. a lot of 15. much, a lot of

Ex. 9, p. 152: 1. many or a lot of 2. many or a lot of 3. much or a lot of, many or a lot of 4. a lot of 5. a lot of 6. a lot of

Ex. 10, p. 153: 1. a little 2. a little 3. a few 4. a little 5. a little 6. a little 7. a few 8. a little 9. a few 10. a few 11. a few 12. a little 13. a few 14. a few 15. a little 16. a few 17. a little 18. a little

Ex. 11, p. 153: 1. a few, a little 2. a few, a little 3. A little, a few 4. a little 5. a few, a few 6. a few, a little, a little

Ex. 12, p. 154: 1. many 2. a little 3. a lot of 4. a

lot of 5. a few 6. much 7. a lot of 8. a lot of 9. a lot of 10. a lot of 11. much, much 12. a lot of

Ex. 13, p. 155: answers will vary

Ex. 14, p. 155: 1. A 2. B 3. D 4. D 5. A 6. B 7. C 8. C

Ex. 15, p. 156: Part 1. 1. some/any, a little, some/any, any, some (or a little) 2. a lot of, many/a lot of 3. many/a lot of 4. some/any, any, some, some, any; Part 2. 1. correct 2. correct 3. wrong (much = a lot of) 4. wrong (a few homeworks = a little homework) 5. correct 6. correct 7. wrong (has beautiful = has a beautiful) 8. wrong (change *some* to *any*)

Unit 11

Ex. 1, p. 161: 1. on 2. at 3. on 4. at 5. on 6. in 7. at 8. at 9. on 10. in 11. at 12. on 13. in 14. on 15. on

Ex. 2, p. 161: 1. on 2. at 3. on 4. at 5. on 6. in 7. at 8. at 9. on 10. in 11. at 12. on 13. in 14. on 15. on

Ex. 3, p. 161: 1. in 2. on 3. in 4. at 5. on 6. in 7. in 8. on 9. on 10. in 11. in 12. at 13. on 14. in 15. in; at + McDonald's, 10 A.M.; on + Main Street, Monday, May 11, Highway 883, your birthday; in + Canada, the kitchen, Paris, the summer, May, 1993, Texas, December; use *at* with business places with names, clock time; use *on* with days and dates, streets (highways); use *in* with countries, rooms, cities, seasons, months, years, states

Ex. 4, p. 162: 1. in 2. on 3. at 4. at 5. at 6. at 7. at 8. on 9. at 10. in 11. in 12. on 13. in 14. at 15. in; at + Burger King, 2127 Hills Street, Hardee's, Bob's Used Cars, noon, Dairy Queen, 7 P.M.; on + September 11, Friday, Cayuga Road; in + Mexico, Panama, Thailand, 1988, 1776; use *at* with business places with names, with specific addresses; use *on* with dates, days, streets (roads); use *in* with countries, years

Ex. 5, p. 163: 1. on, in 2. on 3. at, in 4. In, in 5. at, at 6. in, in 7. on, in 8. in, at 9. at, on 10. at, in

Ex. 6, p. 164: 1. on, in 2. in, in 3. in, in 4. on, in 5. at, at 6. at, at 7. in, in 8. in, at 9. in, on 10. at, on 11. In, in, on

Ex. 7, p. 165:

Vick	1970	Miami	McDonald's	Main Street	7:00 A.M.
Paul	1960	New York	Nation's Bank	Ben Road	9:00 A.M.
Tasha	1975	Atlanta	Delta Airlines	Peach Street	3:00 P.M.
Hank	1963	Dallas	Star Taxi Co.	Coral Street	11:00 P.M.
Marjory	1950	Memphis	Nation's Bank	Branch Road	9:00 A.M.

Ex. 8, p. 166: Group 1. in 1997, at 2 P.M., in the evening, in January, in the kitchen, at First Union Bank, on Miller Road, on Saturday, on the last day, in summer; Group 2. on Monday, on the shelf, in fall, in the afternoon, at 6 A.M., in the bathroom, in 1776, on Young Avenue, at Sam's Market, in December; Group 3. at night, in May, in winter, in 1945, at midnight, on Tuesday, in the bedroom, on Ponte Street, at Pizza Hut, on Friday

Ex. 9, p. 167: 1. D 2. C 3. B 4. A 5. A 6. C 7. B
8. B

Ex. 10, p. 168: Part 1. 1. at, on 2. in, in, in 3. in, at, in, on 4. in, in 5. on; Part 2. 1. wrong (on = in) 2. wrong (in = at) 3. correct 4. correct 5. wrong (in = on) 6. correct 7. correct 8. wrong (on = in) 9. wrong (in = at) 10. wrong (in = at)

Unit 12

Ex. 1, p. 171: 1. doesn't 2. didn't 3. wasn't 4. wasn't 5. isn't 6. wasn't 7. am not 8. didn't 9. don't 10. aren't

Ex. 2, p. 171: answers will vary

Ex. 3, p. 172: Across: 1. A. isn't B. doesn't C. don't 4. A. aren't B. don't C. aren't 6. A. isn't B. doesn't C. isn't 7. A. isn't B. doesn't C. didn't Down: 1. A. isn't B. don't C. doesn't 2. A. don't, don't, isn't 3. A. isn't B. isn't C. isn't 5. A. doesn't B. isn't C. isn't, doesn't 6. A. isn't B. aren't C. doesn't

Ex. 4, p. 173: 1. B 2. A 3. D 4. C 5. A 6. B 7. C 8. D 9. C 10. C 11. A 12. C 13. B 14. C 15. A

Ex. 5, p. 176: answers will vary

Ex. 6, p. 176:

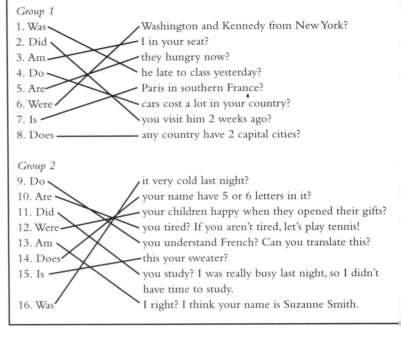

Group 1
1. Was — Washington and Kennedy from New York?
2. Did — I in your seat?
3. Am — they hungry now?
4. Do — he late to class yesterday?
5. Are — Paris in southern France?
6. Were — cars cost a lot in your country?
7. Is — you visit him 2 weeks ago?
8. Does — any country have 2 capital cities?

Group 2
9. Do — it very cold last night?
10. Are — your name have 5 or 6 letters in it?
11. Did — your children happy when they opened their gifts?
12. Were — you tired? If you aren't tired, let's play tennis!
13. Am — you understand French? Can you translate this?
14. Does — this your sweater?
15. Is — you study? I was really busy last night, so I didn't have time to study.
16. Was — I right? I think your name is Suzanne Smith.

Ex. 7, p. 178: 1. Yes, they are./No, they aren't. 2. Yes, it did./No, it didn't. 3. Yes, we do./No, we don't. 4. Yes, it was./No, it wasn't. 5. Yes, it does./No, it doesn't. 6. Yes, you are./No, you aren't. 7. Yes, I did./No, I didn't. (or we did and we didn't) 8. Yes, he is./No, he isn't. 9. Yes, they are./No, they aren't. 10. Yes, we were./No, we weren't.

Ex. 8, p. 179: 1. When did the U.S. become independent? 2. What does stream mean? 3. Why does the teacher arrive early? 4. A. Who invented the lightbulb? B. What did Thomas Edison invent? C. Where was he born? D. When did he die? 5. A. Who wrote a letter to the boy's parents? B. Who(m) did the teacher write a letter to?

Ex. 9, p. 180: 1. this, That, these, Those, Those 2. those, These, that 3. sweaters, sweater

Ex. 10, p. 180: 1. some, some, any 2. some/any, a lot, a few, some 3. some, much/a lot of, much, a few

Ex. 11, p. 181: simple present: every day, sometimes, all the time, usually; simple past: in 1993, yesterday, last night, 5 minutes ago, last month; present progressive: today, right now, this year, at this moment, now, this month

Ex. 12, p. 182: 1. are you doing, am cleaning, listening 2. arrived, walked, was, rained, am watching, is 3. attends, is studying, wants

Ex. 13, p. 183: 1. is 2. owns 3. live 4. is 5. think 6. visit 7. come 8. come 9. means 10. arrived 11. used 12. received

Ex. 14, p. 184: 1. B 2. B 3. A 4. B 5. C 6. D 7. D 8. C

Ex. 15, p. 185: 1. in, on, on 2. in, In, in 3. on, on, in, in 4. in, in, in, in

Crossword grid:
1. T U R T L E / 2. / 3. E
U / E / I
4. E Y E S / G
S / T / H
D / 5. M / 6. I / T
7. A P R I L L
Y / S / L

Final Test

Name_____ Date _____

This test has 22 questions. You will receive 1 point for circling the error and 1 point for correcting the error. Perfect score = 44.

Your score: ____/44 = ____%

(70% minimum recommended for passing)

Each sentence contains one error. Circle the error and write a correction on the line. If your answer is long, you may write it above the sentence.

example: ____have____ I(has)a book.

Part 1

1. _____ The students in my grammar class is from many different countries.

2. _____ I like apples, and Mike like apples, too.

3. _____ Those apples over here look very good.

4. _____ Do they have they're books with them?

5. _____ The apples in the box no were good.

6. _____ I wasn't like onions when I was a child.

7. _____ Who have a red car?

8. _____ The dictionaries are in the room on the table in a box.

9. _____ He listens to music right now.

10. _____ Mr. Paulson doesn't have some coins for the telephone.

11. _____ My brother works in World Trading Company.

Part 2

1. _____ The name of the new store on Main Street Sam's Shirts.

2. _____ Brazil and India don't countries in Africa.

3 _____ Do you like this books very much?

4. _____ Susan left the house, but she book is here on the table.

5. _____ Mark is in Chicago three years ago.

6. _____ The teacher did not attended class yesterday.

7. _____ What can I buy tennis pants and tennis shoes?

8. _____ Were you on Wednesday at the meeting?

9. _____ I can't play tennis now because I study for a test.

10. _____ He has much money, so he's a very rich man.

11. _____ The final exam is in next Tuesday.

Diagnostic Test

Name_____ Date_____

Directions: Mark an X on the letter of the correct answer. Mark all answers on this sheet.

			TEACHER ONLY Number wrong (0, 1, 2)
1a. (A) (B) (C) (D)	1b. (A) (B) (C) (D)		_____
2a. (A) (B) (C) (D)	2b. (A) (B) (C) (D)		_____
3a. (A) (B) (C) (D)	3b. (A) (B) (C) (D)		_____
4a. (A) (B) (C) (D)	4b. (A) (B) (C) (D)		_____
5a. (A) (B) (C) (D)	5b. (A) (B) (C) (D)		_____
6a. (A) (B) (C) (D)	6b. (A) (B) (C) (D)		_____
7a. (A) (B) (C) (D)	7b. (A) (B) (C) (D)		_____
8a. (A) (B) (C) (D)	8b. (A) (B) (C) (D)		_____
9a. (A) (B) (C) (D)	9b. (A) (B) (C) (D)		_____
10a. (A) (B) (C) (D)	10b. (A) (B) (C) (D)		_____
11a. (A) (B) (C) (D)	11b. (A) (B) (C) (D)		_____

Diagnostic Test Questions

1a. "Are you, Jill, and Susan in the same class?"

"Yes, _____."

(A) I am   (C) you are

(B) we are   (D) they are

2a. "I can't spell his name. It's hard."

"Yes, that's true. His last name _____ 12 letters. It only has 11."

(A) don't has   (C) doesn't have

(B) doesn't has   (D) don't have

3a. _____ do not look good together.

(A) These painting and those vase   (C) These painting and that vase

(B) This painting and those vase   (D) This painting and that vase

4a. "Is this a new book?"

"Yes, it is. It's _____ birthday present from John. He gave it to me yesterday."

(A) his   (C) your

(B) my   (D) their

5a. "_____ Paul Johnson in math class yesterday?"

"I'm not sure, but I think he was there."

(A) Is   (C) Does

(B) Was   (D) Did

6a. "Did Luke work with you at First National Bank?"

"Yes, _____."

(A) he did   (C) he was

(B) we did   (D) we were

7a. "What _____?"

"It means very big."

(A) means huge   (C) does mean huge

(B) huge means   (D) does huge mean

8a. We like to write letters. We write _____.

A) every day letters in our room   (C) in our room every day letters

(B) letters every day in our room   (D) letters in our room every day

9a. "_____ Jim and Sam study together every day?"

"No, because they live in different parts of the city."

(A) Are   (C) Is

(B) Do   (D) Does

10a. "Do you like coffee?"

"Oh, yes. I drink _____ coffee every day."

(A) a lot of   (C) many

(B) much   (D) any

11a. "Where do you work?"

"_____ Lucky Travel Agency."

(A) In   (C) On

(B) At   (D) To

1b. "_____ cheap in your country?"

"No, they aren't. They're very expensive."

(A) Cars are   (C) Are cars

(B) Gasoline is   (D) Is gasoline

2b. "_____?"

"No, he doesn't. He isn't a very good student."

(A) Do Tom have a book   (C) Doe he does his homework

(B) Does Tom try hard   (D) Does he studies much

3b. Joe and Sue are in a store. Sue picks up a tennis ball and asks Joe about it.

Sue: "Hey, Joe. What kind of ball is _____?"

Joe: "That's a tennis ball. You don't play tennis?"

(A) this   (C) these

(B) that   (D) those

4b. "I'd like to cash this check, please."

"OK. But I need to see _____ driver' license or some kind of ID."

(A) his   (C) your

(B) my   (D) their

5b. "Were all the answers on your test correct?"

"No, _____. Number 7 was wrong."

(A) they weren't   (C) they aren't

(B) it wasn't   (D) it isn't

6b. "Did she _____ to the meeting yesterday?"

"No, she was sick and stayed home instead."

(A) go   (C) was go

(B) went   (D) going

7b. "_____ did you go there?"

"Because we needed some milk."

(A) When   (C) What

(B) Where   (D) Why

8b. He goes _____ every day.

(A) at 8 to the bank   (C) in the morning early

(B) to the library at noon   (D) on Martin Street to the store

9b. "Where is Kevin?"

"He's at Greg's house. They _____ football."

(A) are playing   (C) playing

(B) is playing   (D) play

10b. "Is there anything on the table?"

"Yes, there is a _____."

(A) notebooks   (C) magazine

(B) dictionaries   (D) slices of pie

11b. "Let's play tennis at _____."

"OK, that sounds like a good idea to me."

(A) 10:30   (C) the afternoon

(B) Tuesday   (D) April 20